Alia and Radwa have created a masterpiece debut cookbook. They effortlessly teach that food can be delicious, healthy, and beautiful, even when life is hectic. I'll be dreaming about their lemon ricotta pancakes until further notice!

—Giada De Laurentiis

I have been a fan of Alia and Radwa's for quite some time. Their fun approach to food and their connection to their roots is what drew me in—and their first cookbook gives the reader just that: beautiful Mediterranean recipes that you can easily re-create in your own kitchen. That's *Pretty Delicious,* if you ask me.

—Tiffani Thiessen, actress and cookbook author of *Here We Go Again* and *Pull Up a Chair*

This book is truly a magical gateway to a world of deliciousness and a perfect introduction for those excited to learn more about Mediterranean, Middle Eastern, and Egyptian cuisines. The recipes are an ideal combination of new and classic flavors, and each photo is stunning. I am sure you will enjoy every bite!

—Betül Tunç, baker and author of *Turkuaz Kitchen*

Alia and [...] ing mission: to make life easier one recipe at a time. With *Pretty Delicious,* they expanded that idea into a simple and insanely flavorful way to cook with all of my favorite Mediterranean, Egyptian, and Levant-centric flavors. Enjoy the culture trip from Food Dolls, and don't sleep on that fava bean salad or tahini ice cream, either.

—Andrew Zimmern, traveler, chef, writer, and teacher

Alia and Radwa have created a gorgeous collection of recipes for every mood and time of day that is both accessible and beautiful. The Double-Duty Dips chapter is worth buying the book for alone . . . what wouldn't you want to put Roasted-Tomato Baba G or Baba's Tahina Sauce on? *Pretty Delicious* will inspire you to plant your Mediterranean roots—and have great fun doing it.

—Kat Ashmore, creator of Kat Can Cook and *New York Times* bestselling author of *Big Bites*

Pretty
Delicious

Pretty
Delicious

SIMPLE, MODERN MEDITERRANEAN, SERVED WITH STYLE

Alia Elkaffas & Radwa Elkaffas

creators of FOOD DOLLS

with Rachel Holtzman

Photographs by Eva Kolenko

CLARKSON POTTER
PUBLISHERS
New York

who always gather the family around the dinner table. We hope to continue making you proud. We love you with all of our hearts.

Contents

What's for Dinner?

Pretty Sweet

All Dolled Up

Introduction

We like to say that our cooking and lifestyle platform, Food Dolls, was built from one simple question: *What are* you *making for dinner?* For as long as we can remember, we've always done what sisters do best: talk for hours on the phone about anything and everything—our latest Home Goods scores (Another day, another serving board!), what we're wearing to the next date night with our husbands or girls' night out (Jeans, cute top, and heels? Classic for a reason!), our most exciting Amazon finds (Hot pink fluffy slides? Immediately, yes.), and our shared obsessions over the perfect white paint (Benjamin Moore White Dove), bold lipstick (Ladies Night by Huda Beauty), and *all* the clear organizing containers. But about seven years ago, when Alia found her days consumed by raising three young boys and Radwa had just had her first daughter, many of those check-ins centered around one reality we had to face every single day—someone had to get dinner on the table, and that someone was going to be *us*.

Growing up, we were always encouraged by our mom to get into the kitchen on Sundays to help her to cook. We are, after all, part of a big Egyptian family whose livelihood revolves around food (think *My Big Fat Greek Wedding* but with more shawarma and less Windex). Mom was the original meal prepper. She and our dad both worked full-time, so once a week, she'd spend several hours setting herself up for a week's worth of homemade lunches and dinners. When we were little, we loved making traditional Egyptian dishes like kofta (page 205), koshari (page 149), and kunafa (page 245) while we chatted and laughed and our mom taught us her signature laid-back approach of "a little bit of this, a little bit of that." Eventually, life got in the way (hanging out with friends, getting our nails done, going to the movies . . . basically anything *but* cooking)—until it came time to start our own families. But even then, we still weren't interested in spending hours in our kitchens the way our mom did. (No offense, Mama!) Instead, we started looking to the newly created "Food Tok" for fast and easy weeknight meal inspiration. The only problem was that we still had trouble finding recipes that sounded good to us. They either weren't very healthy (we're both big fans of the 80/20 rule—eating mostly whole-ingredient, veg-forward meals but also leaving room for things like Baklava Cinnamon Rolls, page 35, and Turkish Coffee Tiramisu, page 235), were too complicated to make while dragging a small child around the kitchen or running into the house after work, weren't very polished (a quick meal doesn't have to look or taste like it!), or didn't have the same vibrant and complex flavors of our favorite Mediterranean and Middle Eastern dishes. So even though we had no idea *how* we'd actually accomplish it, we both came to the same conclusion: We can do it better.

At first, we didn't know how it would go over, introducing people to dishes like Whipped Feta with roasted tomatoes and chickpeas or Sumac Chicken Wings alongside things like one-pot Spicy Rigatoni and Strawberry-Mascarpone Stuffed-Croissant French Toast (we are also, after all, a couple of Minnesota girls). But as it turns out, our followers are just as hungry as we are for quick and simple meets fresh and new. And it's clear they love both our traditional preparations in addition to updated Mediterranean and Middle Eastern-ish spins on classics, like Baklava Cinnamon Rolls, Chicken Kofta Burgers, and Steak Shawarma Bowls.

Our community now tells us in no uncertain terms that our signature Food Dolls approach to preparing meals is working—and we're not just talking about how they love the way we finish each other's sentences in our videos in true sister-telepathy style or how we never pretend that we always have it all together ourselves (because we don't!). Aside from that, we hear again and again how we've been able to help solve real-life problems for cooks, from newlyweds to new parents, to people who are new to the kitchen and don't know where to start. What we all have in common is that we want a go-to stash of works-every-time recipes that don't *feel* like the same-old same-old. And because we love entertaining so much, we also offer fun, polished ways to gather with friends and family that don't require a ton of work or expense. In *Pretty Delicious,* our very first (!) cookbook, we are so excited to share our tried-and-true hacks and shortcuts, so many pantry staples to play with, dozens of dishes that hit the perfect mark between indulgent and nourishing, and beautiful presentations that don't take much extra effort. In short: modernized traditions for the real world. And that's what this book is all about.

We're writing *Pretty Delicious* with the same mission we've had since Day 1: "Making life easier, one recipe at a time." That's right; when it comes to getting breakfast, lunch, dinner, and even special-occasion meals on the table, we have you covered. But just because we're saving you time, money, and sanity doesn't mean these recipes are anything short of crave-worthy. We're talking Crispy Baked Halloumi with Hot Honey Drizzle (page 74), Middle Eastern–Style Beef Pot Roast (page 210—or Pomegranate Molasses Carrots with Chickpeas and Couscous on page 169 for anyone who wants to keep it veg), Shrimp Tagine with Garlicky Tomatoes and Peppers (page 180), and No-Churn Salted Tahini Cookies 'n' Cream Ice Cream (page 236). Basically, we've taken some of our favorite Middle Eastern family dishes, added some casseroles, icebox cakes, and other old-school favorites—because you can't take the girls out of the Midwest—and we've updated them for the way people cook now: fewer ingredients and steps, while being healthier and offering *much* more interesting flavors. As we like to say at the end of all our recipe videos: *Yessss!*

We also believe that our meals should feel as good to prep and make as they are to eat. Does that mean we think you should spend a bunch of time in the kitchen and love every minute of it? Um, no. We can think of one hundred other things we either need or want to be doing rather than endlessly prepping meals most days. But we have figured out that if you have a well-stocked refrigerator and pantry and make-ahead meals ready to grab, then suddenly pulling together something to eat doesn't feel like a chore—and the meals themselves seem even more effortless and elevated.

Last but not least, we want to show you how meals can feel polished and put-together, even when you're juggling that third load of laundry and carpool pickup. Whether you're cooking for immediate family or a book club, we've got you covered with how to actually get a meal on the table (and look cute doing it!). No matter how casual or special the occasion, we'll take you through the basics of styling a table (a theme and a few great serving pieces go a long way!), how to put together a menu (including sample menus to get started), and tips for how to prep ahead so you can actually enjoy yourself when it's time to eat. From a teatime tray (page 271) to a buffet (page 277) suitable for your enormous Egyptian family (or any regular family!), to our famous no-cook dessert bar cart (page 278), we've got all the inspo you need to feel confident when it comes to entertaining—and we promise, it won't require much more than a few of our tasty, dependable, inexpensive recipes.

We hope that through the recipes here, cooking breakfast, lunch, and dinner will become less of a need-to and more of a want-to. We *know* the days when it feels like there's barely any time left for you, and yet we also know how good it is to share a delicious meal, tuck into a beautifully layered jar of salad (when you otherwise would have settled for a handful of cookies), or feel totally victorious upon opening your pantry and only needing a quick trip to the store to make an entire week's worth of meals.

Our goal is to meet you where life is, in all of its unpredictable, chaotic, messy glory. We're here for you every step of the way, with all the mouthwatering inspiration, foolproof recipes, and time-saving shortcuts we can possibly put together. And, at the end of the day, we'd like to think the only difficult part of *What are you making for dinner?* is choosing which dish to cook up first. Here's to making real life a little prettier and a lot more delicious!

XO,

Alia + Dadra

Make Your Kitchen Your Happy Place

When we created Food Dolls, our two main goals were to help people spend less time in the kitchen cooking for their families, while also making the time they spend in the kitchen even more enjoyable. After years of experimenting with how to find that sweet spot ourselves, we've discovered that it comes down to a few steps:

GEAR UP

Having the right tools and equipment for cooking a variety of dishes and making prep as efficient as possible.

GET ORGANIZED

Keeping our kitchen spaces (especially the fridge and pantry) organized so we can see what we have, avoid double-purchasing, and feel generally less overwhelmed by clutter.

GET CUTE

Adding personal aesthetic touches that make the kitchen feel like the kind of place we want to be in. If we're going to be in there every day, it might as well be nice to look at!

STEP 1: Gear Up

Before you read this section and start loading up your shopping cart at your favorite online retailer (you know the one we're talking about!), keep in mind that you most likely already have many of these things. First, take an inventory of what's already in your cabinets and make a wish list of what you still need. Then, over time, collect items as you're able to, especially when these items are on sale or marked down for promotions (as all almost always eventually are).

CUTTING AND CHOPPING

Chef's knife: Invest in a large (we like 8-inch) high-quality knife that you can use for all your prep work. While many kitchen items that you buy do not need to be top-tier, a chef's knife is worth spending a little more on (our favorite brand is Zwilling). That said, a middle-of-the-road knife will serve you just fine so long as you keep it sharp.

Paring knife: This is good for smaller cutting tasks, such as peeling and trimming.

Kitchen shears: Use these for trimming herbs, opening packaging, or breaking down poultry.

Knife sharpener: This is important for keeping your knives and kitchen shears sharp for safe and efficient cooking. We like a four-stage pull-through sharpener.

Vegetable chopper: This handy tool helps cut everything uniformly and reduces prep time by more than half—we think it's a must-have. Make sure to get one that's dishwasher-safe, large enough to accommodate the chopping you need, has large and small dice options, and can double as a spiralizer and/or julienne veggies.

Garlic press: A must, in our opinion—it makes mincing garlic *much* more efficient.

Cutting boards: In order to prevent cross-contamination, we recommend getting two—one for meat, poultry, and seafood, and the other for fruits and vegetables. We tend to avoid wood cutting boards for anything other than charcuterie because they need some extra TLC such as regular oiling to keep them from drying out or absorbing odors. That's why we prefer plastic or vinyl because they're dishwasher-safe, don't absorb odors, and are easily sanitized. Look for a board that's large enough for you to do all your food prep but still fits comfortably on your countertop or in your sink for cleaning. Thicker boards tend to be sturdier, and nonslip feet or grips are always a plus. See Get Cute (page 23) for more recommendations on how these everyday items can do double-duty as decor.

PREPARATION AND MIXING

Measuring cups and spoons: You'll need cups for liquid and dry.

Vegetable peeler: We like the Oxo swivel peeler.

Box grater

Salad spinnner

Microplane rasp grater: The long and narrow one.

Pepper grinder: Most of our recipes call for freshly ground black pepper, which has a more interesting spicy, almost floral flavor compared to preground pepper. Plus it's a functional item that can add personality to your table (see page 23).

Whisk: A metal balloon whisk will work for most applications, but a silicone-covered whisk is great for nonstick pans.

Wooden spoon and spatula: These are gentle on cookware and ideal for stirring and flipping.

Slotted spoon: Helpful for scooping and straining items out of liquid.

Tongs

Ladle

Silicone, rubber, or heatproof spatula

Metal spatula

Colander

Mixing bowls: It can be helpful to have small, medium, and large options.

ON THE STOVE
AND IN THE OVEN

Sheet pans: A large one (also called a half-sheet pan) that fits in your oven can be used for all your roasting and baking needs. It's also nice to have a smaller (quarter-sheet) option for when you want to halve recipes or only have a small number of items that need roasting or baking.

Casserole/baking dishes: A 7 × 11-inch, 9 × 13-inch, or 8 × 12-inch baking dish plus 2- and 3-quart casserole dishes will suit a wide variety of dishes. We also like having a 9 × 9-inch baking dish to change things up, as well an oval baker because it looks pretty on the table.

Dutch oven and large stockpot: We reach for a large soup pot when making soup or boiling pasta, and grab a Dutch oven—a pot that can go from stove to oven—for pretty much everything else. We love enamel-coated Dutch ovens because they retain heat so well and are fairly nonstick, too.

Saucepan with a fitted lid: A medium-sized (2-quart) option is great for making rice, sauces, grains, and soups.

Large skillets: We like having both a nonstick and stainless steel 12-inch option. Stainless steel offers the best heat distribution and retention, while nonstick pans make cooking and cleanup a lot easier. Both will last for a very long time with proper care (i.e., no sticking them in the dishwasher!).

A digital/instant-read thermometer

Oven mitts or potholders

STEP 2: Get Organized

Listen, we've had to stare down a deep, dark cabinet stuffed to bursting with items from more years than we care to admit. And we, too, have gone through survival-mode stretches where things get jammed into the fridge every which way and condiments linger past their welcome. But what became clear as we started cooking every day was that we looked forward to it more when ingredients were easily at hand. Being organized means you don't constantly second-guess yourself whether something is stocked or not, and you don't end up staring down twenty-five bottles of just-opened salad dressing every time you open the fridge (especially because we learned that they are a million times better when we make them ourselves!). Getting your pantry in order can certainly feel like a giant chore, but if you take it one step at a time and maintain the order as best you can, you'll get to experience the unparalleled satisfaction of walking into your kitchen and knowing that everything is exactly where it should be.

HOW WE ORGANIZE OUR PANTRY

Take everything out: We mean *everything*. Every drawer, every cabinet. Put all the contents on the counter—we guarantee you that you'll find at least a few surprises, so do yourself a favor and don't skip this step.

Declutter: Before we even attempt to organize, we first get rid of items that are expired, stale, a duplicate, or no longer regularly used in our house. If an item is still sealed and not expired, we donate it to a local food pantry.

Maximize your space: Now that your storage space is empty, assess whether you're using it optimally. Consider adding shelf dividers and/or adjustable shelves, a lazy Susan, or pull-out drawers (which are especially great for deeper cabinets). If you have a tall pantry, you can install hooks or pegs to hang items like aprons, oven mitts, or reusable grocery bags. (S-hooks are especially great for these.)

Group similar items: Categorize your remaining items into groups such as pasta, canned goods, baking supplies, snacks, etc. Storing these things together will make it easier for you to find what you need. When these items go back into the pantry, they become "zones," which helps streamline your process. You can get as creative as you want, as long as it's genuinely helpful for you. One of our favorite personalized zones is a breakfast station, or a shelf dedicated to things like cereals, oatmeal, pancake mix, and syrup, which truly makes busy mornings easier.

Use magazine holders for wraps and foils: Our favorite hack for keeping these things tidy and easy to grab.

Lighting: If your pantry lacks good lighting, consider installing LED strip lights or battery-powered motion-sensor lights to make it easier to see everything.

Add a step stool: If you have high shelves, keep a stool nearby for easier access.

Keep things clear: We recommend using clear and airtight storage containers for things like flour, sugar, pasta, rice, and grains, as well as clear bins for snacks and small items like spice jars and packets to keep them from getting lost and to make things look nice and neat. Now you'll always know what you have and how much is left.

Add labels: This helps both you and your family keep track of what's what, as well as put things back where they belong. For bulk items, it can be useful to add an expiration date as well.

Prioritize accessibility: Keep your most frequently used items at eye level and within easy reach. Items you only use every once in a while can be stored higher or lower. That said, snacks are best kept where kids can reach them!

Create a first-in-first-out system: When restocking your pantry, put new items behind older ones. This helps ensure that you use items before they expire. If using canisters for bulk staples like flour and sugar, wait until the containers are empty before refilling them.

Maintain a shopping list: Keep a small whiteboard or notepad in your pantry to jot down items that need to be replaced. This way, you can avoid overbuying and know what you need when you go shopping. Just don't forget to take a photo of it before heading to the store!

Don't overstock: While it's helpful to have a well-stocked pantry, don't overdo it. Overcrowding can lead to disorganization and waste. Use up what you have and buy what you need as you need it.

Regularly check and rotate items: Periodically check for soon-to-expire items and use them in your meals. This keeps your pantry fresh and reduces waste.

list continues >

HOW WE ORGANIZE
OUR FRIDGE

Clean and clear: Similarly to organizing the pantry (see page 19), always begin with a good cleaning. Start by taking everything out and wiping down the shelves and drawers. Most of these pieces can be removed from the refrigerator completely, which we highly recommend you do. Throw away all expired items, as well as items you know in your heart you'll never use again. Let it go!

Create zones: Designate specific areas of the fridge for different categories of food. For example:

Top shelf: ready-to-eat and leftover foods

Middle shelves: beverages, homemade condiments, and dairy products (the temperature is most consistent in this part of the fridge, which is optimal for things like eggs and milk)

Bottom shelf: meat and seafood

Drawers: fruits and vegetables

Door: store-bought condiments and frequently used items

Clear it up: Consider adding clear storage containers for items like deli meats, cheeses, and leftovers. Label and date the containers to keep track of their freshness. You can also use bins to keep like items together, such as snacks and beverages.

Keep a rotation: Place newer items at the back of the fridge and move older items to the front to ensure that you use them before they expire.

Reduce clutter: Store only what you need and will use in the near future.

Adjust temperature settings: Make sure that your fridge is set at the right temperature (around 37°F) to keep your food fresh. Use a refrigerator thermometer to monitor the temperature.

Don't forget about the freezer: The same steps above apply here. Also, make sure to periodically defrost and clean your freezer to prevent ice buildup. We like to do this about every other month—but we're extra like that! Aim for at least once a year.

THE SPICE CABINET

Since we'll be introducing you to a number of new spices, you'll want to make sure that your spice cabinet is also in order.

If you want to add your spices to clear bottles or jars that you'll label, here's how:

Start with small glass jars or containers with airtight lids. We use 8-ounce jars because we go through *a lot* of spices, but you could also use 4- or 6-ounce jars. Make sure they are clean and dry in order to ensure that your spices are potent and fresh for as long as possible.

Based on your inventory of your spices (after you've decluttered!), create labels for each bottle. We like using a label maker, but you could also purchase premade labels, or find blank adhesive labels and customize them with a permanent marker. You'll also want to include an expiration date. Ground spices will keep fresh for 6 months, and whole spices can last for up to 1 year. If you get down to the dregs of a spice jar and need to refill, be sure to pour off the remaining spice into a bowl first, add the fresh spice to the container, then top off with the old.

Carefully decant your spices into the jars. A funnel comes in handy here. If you have leftover spices, do what our mom taught us and store them in the freezer so they stay fresh.

Optimize the space of your spice drawer or corner of your pantry by using drawer inserts, tiered shelving, or a lazy Susan. Or you could corral them in small clear bins, which helps keep the bottles from tipping. You can organize your spices alphabetically, but you could also do it by color, type, or frequency of use.

Get Cute

At first glance, you wouldn't necessarily think styling your kitchen has anything to do with making great meals for your family, but we think they go hand in hand. It doesn't have to cost a lot of money to make your kitchen feel special, and yet just a few simple touches can elevate your kitchen into a room you really want to spend time in. And the happier you are in your kitchen, the better your food will taste—it's just a fact. Here's how we add style, warmth, and personality to our space while still prioritizing functionality:

Color palette: When choosing new items for your kitchen (whether decor, gadgets, or cookware), coordinate them with your kitchen's existing color scheme to make things feel cohesive.

Open shelving: If you have the wall space, adding shelves to display colorful dishes, mugs, and kitchen accessories adds a touch of charm while also making these things easily accessible.

Dish towels: This is your permission to retire dish towels that are stained, full of holes, and no longer bring you joy. If you can, donate them somewhere that can recycle them. Then refresh your collection with others that complement your kitchen's color palette. They're as decorative as they are useful!

Cabinet knobs and pulls: The easiest way to upgrade your cabinetry is to give the hardware a refresh, whether you want a more vintage vibe, charming shapes, or modern metal. Many of them can simply be removed with a screwdriver.

Plants and flowers: Fresh flowers are the quickest way to give your kitchen warmth and style. Choose varieties that match your kitchen's color scheme and style (our personal favorite is hydrangeas) and display them in a vase or decorative container on your kitchen island, countertop, windowsill, or table. Be sure to change the water regularly to get the most mileage. Potted plants in a variety of sizes can also add that same liveliness to the space.

Decorative plates and platters: Hanging these on the wall is an easy and inexpensive way to create kitchen "art."

Kitchen gadgets and appliances: These days, almost anything you can buy for your kitchen comes in multiple colors. We are *not* suggesting you replace what you already have; rather, we suggest considering your kitchen's palette and style when buying upgrades. For us, that's modern stainless and black, but for you it might be bold gem-tones, neutrals, or soft pastels.

Glass jars and canisters: Your storage can double as decor! Pasta, legumes, flour, sugar, spices—when uniform, neatly labeled, and arranged on open shelving, it doesn't get more chic *or* functional.

Cozy touches: If your kitchen has seating, add cushions and throw pillows to make it more inviting and comfortable.

Linens and rugs: Tablecloths, placemats, and kitchen rugs are all ways to bring in more color, pattern, and texture. And the best part is that there are tons of options for affordable and stylish versions.

Table settings: There's no quicker and easier way to elevate an everyday meal than with tableware that feels special. We're not talking fine china here; rather, dinner plates and silverware that genuinely bring you joy and work with your kitchen's aesthetic. For fancier occasions—or just-because moments—break out the chargers and candle holders!

Salt and pepper shakers: If they're going to be on the table, they might as well be cute! They come in a wide range of colors, materials, and styles to suit your kitchen's color scheme and style.

Cutting boards: These can be decorative elements, too! Whether you gravitate toward rustic wood slabs, modern marble, or bolder patterns and prints, you can lean them against the backsplash in ascending order of size, or hang them on the wall with small hooks.

Cookbooks: If you keep your cookbooks in the kitchen, you can organize them by color for a more cohesive look. We like to keep ours in several smaller stacks around the kitchen so they don't take up too much space while also adding additional pops of color and interest.

list continues >

Soft lighting: The kitchen is an actual room in your house—you should treat it like one! As in, it can have the same lighting considerations as other rooms you love to spend time in, like your living or family room. Yes, you'll need brighter overhead lights for when you're prepping, but for moments when you're eating, cleaning up, or just spending time with your family, you can switch to lamps, or see if you can have an electrician add a dimmer to your existing overhead lighting.

Candles: There's no quicker way to make a space feel warm and inviting than with candles. They can stand on their own as pillars or tea lights, sit together in groups (which always looks stylish), or be placed in candle holders or candelabra (a fun way to add a little drama). You can also add scented candles; just opt for scents that aren't too overpowering and make sense in a space where you eat, such as vanilla or citrus.

Seasonal decorations: Nothing makes the kitchen more festive than holiday- or season-specific elements that you can change out throughout the year. Once you start your collection, you can store seasonal items for the following year so you aren't always needing to accumulate more things.

Coffee station: Simply by arranging all your coffee-making essentials in one place, you are creating an inviting—and aesthetically pleasing—element in your kitchen. Start with a tray that fits your space (we like taking advantage of a part of the countertop that's not in the way of meal prep), then add your coffee maker, coffee grinder, mugs, flavored syrups (we like to decant ours into labeled clear containers with easy-pour spouts), and sugars and sweeteners (in small bowls, canisters, or jars, plus tongs or spoons).

Bar cart: We love a cart moment, especially because small, tiered carts are inexpensive, don't take up a lot of space, and can be wheeled to wherever you need them. If you're a cocktail lover, keep yours stocked with glassware, decanters, and a variety of spirits.

Kitchen island centerpiece: One of our signature touches when decorating the kitchen is adding something that draws the eye into the room. Sometimes it's a group of vases of differing heights filled with flowers (fresh or faux), sometimes it's candles in a variety of sizes, and sometimes it's a mix of the two. It instantly looks architectural and expensive—even when it's really (really) not. We recommend corralling everything on a pretty tray, which not only ties everything together visually, but also makes it easier to move when you need the space. This would also work on a kitchen table if your kitchen doesn't have an island or you want to double down on focal-point moments— no such thing as too much!

Ingredient Glossary

We pride ourselves on creating simple recipes that taste impressive yet take little effort to make. One of the secrets to doing that is using spices and other staple ingredients that add complex layers of flavor. For us, these ingredients are pulled directly from the dishes we grew up eating and are mainstays in Mediterranean and Middle Eastern cooking. Most of them you can find at your usual grocery store, and some you may need to grab from a Middle Eastern market or online—such as the spices, which we get from Penzey's because they're such great quality—but all of them are inexpensive, last for a long time if stored properly, and instantly level up even the most straightforward dishes. Since many of them may be new to you, we wanted to give some insight into what they are and what they taste like.

Aleppo pepper: These flakes have a slightly fruity, smoky heat that's similar in spice to a mild jalapeño. Red pepper flakes, which are a bit spicier, are a decent alternative, but the flavor of Aleppo pepper is pretty special, so it's worth tracking down.

Allspice: This spice is actually a dried berry, and tastes like a pungent blend of cloves, cinnamon, and nutmeg. We use it a lot, but you'll notice that it's always with a sparing hand.

Green cardamom: Whether used as whole pods or ground, cardamom is earthy and floral and adds a really interesting bright note to sweet preparations as well as coffee.

Cinnamon: Yes, we know you most likely are familiar with this spice from its sweet applications, but in Middle Eastern cooking it frequently pops up in savory dishes, too. It lends a warm note that brings balance and instant coziness.

Cloves: Similar to cinnamon, this warm spice can go sweet or savory and makes dishes taste sultry and complex.

Coriander: This is actually the seed of the cilantro plant (also referred to as fresh coriander). When used whole or ground, it has a citrusy, earthy flavor.

Cumin: A sweet, nutty, smoky, warm spice that we use *a lot*, both in its ground and whole-seed forms. Because we use it so frequently, we buy ours in bulk from Penzey's online. Good cumin has a strong earthy, peppery aroma.

Ghee: This is clarified butter, meaning the milk solids have been strained out. It has a mild, rich flavor and can be used exactly as you would butter or cooking oil. Because the milk solids have been removed, it has a higher smoke point, making it great for sautéing, pan-frying, and using in Middle Eastern desserts, such as kunafa and baklava. It can also be stored in the pantry rather than the fridge.

list continues >

Harissa paste: A North African chile paste that's spiced but not necessarily spicy (though you can find mild and spicy varieties). You can spoon it as is over savory dishes or use it in a marinade.

Pomegranate molasses: This tart, syrupy reduction of pomegranate juice is like a slightly sweeter, fruitier balsamic glaze. It adds brightness and dimension to anything it's drizzled over.

Sumac: Ground sumac, which is the form we usually use it in, comes from a berry and has a bright, almost lemony flavor. If you can't find sumac, you could use lemon zest as a substitute.

Tahini: Made from ground sesame seeds, its supreme toasty creaminess is a condiment on its own and can add richness and body to a dish. It's also the base of things like tahina sauce, hummus, and baba ghanoush.

Za'atar: This is one of the signature spice blends of the Mediterranean and Middle East and features wild oregano, sesame seeds, and thyme. It's earthy and savory and adds sparkle to whatever it's sprinkled into or onto. It's also delicious swirled into olive oil and used as a dip for warm bread.

Seven Spice:
Also known as Lebanese seven spice, this is sort of the greatest hits of Middle Eastern spices, including cinnamon, coriander, cumin, and cloves. The exact ingredients and ratios will differ depending on where you buy it, but the general idea is always about the same. Be sure to check if the blend you buy includes salt and pepper; if so, you'll want to omit the salt and pepper that these recipes call for. If you're having trouble finding seven spice, you could also make your own (see ingredients at right) and store it as you would any other spices.

Homemade Seven Spice

2 tablespoons ground cumin

1 tablespoon freshly ground black pepper

1 tablespoon ground allspice

2 teaspoons ground cinnamon

2 teaspoons ground cardamom

1 teaspoon ground nutmeg

½ teaspoon ground cloves

Tips for Real Life

Throughout this book, you'll see our Tips for Real Life, which are shortcuts, shopping suggestions, swaps, and all kinds of other helpful tools to make cooking these recipes easy and versatile. In other words, perfectly suited for real life. Here are a few universal tips that will also come in handy:

- **Dry-toasting:** We frequently call for toasting nuts, seeds, and spices in order to release their natural oils and get even more flavor from them. To do this, spread them in a dry pan over low heat. Toast until fragrant, 1 to 2 minutes, then transfer them to a plate and set aside to cool.
- **Multitasking:** Whenever a recipe calls for marinating meat, we like to use that downtime to prep the condiments and sauces we're planning to serve that dish with.

- **Preparing rice and grains:** We love enjoying many of these dishes with a grain such as rice or quinoa. As much as we'd love to say that we have a generations-old recipe for these things, we usually make them according to the package instructions. Be sure to rinse your rice thoroughly—until the water runs clear—before cooking it, which will ensure that it doesn't get gummy.
- **Warming pitas:** Whenever you're enjoying store-bought pita with a dish—which we often do—or using

them to make a pita pocket, you'll have an easier time stuffing them and get more flavor out of them if you warm them first. Wrap them in a slightly damp kitchen towel and microwave on high for 15 seconds. You could also warm them in the oven on a baking sheet at 350°F for 4 to 5 minutes.
- **Freezing leftovers:** We know how valuable freezer space is, which is why whenever we freeze leftovers, we pack them up in large freezer-safe zip-top bags (after letting the food cool to room temperature), press out as much air as possible (to help prevent freezer burn), and lay the bag flat in the freezer.

Breakfast, Brunch, *or* Anytime

For us Egyptians, breakfast is serious business. When we were growing up, our morning meal was often savory and substantial, whether it was spice-infused, olive oil–slicked Turkish eggs; dense, moist falafel and tahina sauce; hearty ful medames; or fresh tomatoes and feta. To this day, these dishes remind us of lazy Saturday mornings when our biggest decision was whether we should spend the day at the mall or the movie theater. And now that we have families of our own, we've continued the tradition of filling bellies with a nourishing breakfast. We've included many of the classics in this chapter, but have also added plenty of options for even quicker meals, many of which can be made in advance (think baked oatmeal, croissant French toast, and chia pudding). Whether you're rushing out the door, enjoying a sleep-in, hosting a brunch, or just in the mood for breakfast—no matter the time of day— these recipes will have the cereal aisle wondering where you disappeared to.

Marinated Tomatoes with Whipped Feta Yogurt

When we were growing up, each weekend without fail, gibna bil tomatim graced our table and to this day it reminds us of lazy Saturday mornings with our family. Literally translating to "cheese and tomatoes," it's a combination of fresh, juicy tomatoes and salty cheese. It's traditionally prepared with domiati, a slightly salty brined cheese made from cow's and sometimes water buffalo's milk, that gets smashed and mixed with the tomatoes—but since we can't get that in Minnesota (yet!) we use feta instead. We wanted to make this dish even more of a morning main event, so we call for whipping the feta with yogurt and heaping it with marinated tomatoes tossed with tons of fresh herbs. Enjoy it on its own; add an egg or two; offer slabs of warm pita, crackers, or crudités for dipping; or serve it alongside your favorite savory breakfast dishes for a brunch-worthy spread.

SERVES 4

MARINATED TOMATOES

2 cups grape tomatoes, quartered

¼ cup finely chopped fresh flat-leaf parsley leaves

¼ cup chopped fresh mint leaves

¼ cup chopped fresh basil leaves

3 tablespoons extra-virgin olive oil

½ teaspoon fine sea salt

¼ teaspoon freshly ground black pepper

WHIPPED FETA YOGURT

6 ounces brine-packed feta cheese, drained (see Tip) and crumbled

½ cup whole-milk plain yogurt

FOR SERVING

Good extra-virgin olive oil, for drizzling

Pita, crackers, or crudités (optional)

MARINATE THE TOMATOES: In a medium bowl, combine the tomatoes, parsley, mint, basil, olive oil, salt, and pepper. Give everything a toss until well combined and let the mixture marinate for at least 15 minutes for the flavors to meld. You could let it sit overnight, covered, in the refrigerator, but hold off on adding the salt or your tomatoes will get soggy.

MEANWHILE, PREPARE THE WHIPPED FETA YOGURT: In a blender, combine the feta with the yogurt and ¼ cup water. Blend until smooth and creamy. If needed, add a bit more water to thin out the mixture to your desired consistency (we like it nice and thick).

TO SERVE: Spoon the whipped feta yogurt into a serving dish. Drain the tomatoes from the bowl, leaving the liquid behind, and spread them over the feta. Finish with a drizzle of olive oil. If desired, serve with pita, crackers, or crudités.

MAKE IT AHEAD

You can make the whipped feta yogurt in advance and store it in an airtight container in the refrigerator for up to 3 days. It's really good on its own as a dip!

Tip for Real Life

Save the brine from the feta to add to a salad dressing or use in a marinade for chicken—the brine adds amazing depth of flavor and helps tenderize the meat.

Baklava Cinnamon Rolls

It's no secret how much we love rich, syrupy, nutty baklava (check out our favorite baklava-inspired treat on page 232). So it seemed only right that we figure out how to eat it for breakfast, too. We like to think that the genius part of this recipe is that it replaces the phyllo with store-bought cinnamon roll dough. When stuffed with a cinnamon-scented walnut and pistachio filling and drizzled with a brown sugar–honey syrup, it's nothing short of dessert-worthy—and yet completely breakfast-appropriate.

SERVES 10

Softened unsalted butter, for the cake pan

SYRUP

¾ cup packed light brown sugar

¾ cup heavy cream

½ cup honey

5 tablespoons unsalted butter

FILLING

⅓ cup walnuts

¼ cup pistachios

2 tablespoons granulated sugar

½ teaspoon ground cinnamon

ASSEMBLY

2 (17.5-ounce) cans cinnamon rolls

Preheat the oven to 350°F. Grease a round 12- or 14-inch cake pan with butter.

MAKE THE SYRUP: In a medium pot, combine the brown sugar, cream, honey, and butter. Bring the ingredients to a boil over medium heat, stirring occasionally. Reduce to a simmer and cook, stirring occasionally, until the sugar has completely dissolved, about 5 minutes. Remove the pot from the heat and set aside.

MAKE THE FILLING: In a food processor, combine the walnuts, pistachios, granulated sugar, and cinnamon. Pulse just until the mixture is coarsely ground. (Making it too sandy or fine will cause it to burn in the oven.)

TO ASSEMBLE: Pop open the can of cinnamon roll dough and unroll on a cutting board or clean work surface, keeping the slices intact so you have a sheet of dough. Spoon one-quarter of the nut filling over each of the rolls. Carefully roll the dough back up as tightly as possible.

Spoon half of the syrup mixture into the bottom of the prepared cake pan. Separate the nut-filled cinnamon rolls and arrange them on top of the syrup in the baking dish, cut-side down. Sprinkle the remaining nut mixture over the rolls. Measure out ½ cup of the syrup and set aside for serving. Drizzle the remaining syrup mixture over the top.

Bake the cinnamon rolls until they are golden brown and fluffy, 38 to 40 minutes.

Let the rolls stand in the baking dish for 5 minutes before removing. Serve warm with a drizzle of the syrup.

Store leftovers in an airtight container in the refrigerator for up to 1 week.

Banana-Bread Baked Oatmeal Three Ways

FAN
FAV

Sometimes survival is the name of the breakfast game. As much as we love the convenience of instant oatmeal packets, we find them lacking in flavor and texture. That's why we came up with this baked version, which can be prepped the night before and baked off in the morning for a hearty, warm breakfast. We've included three kid-requested, mom-approved versions: the original, which truly tastes like banana bread in oatmeal form, and two variations. There is a double-chocolate variation and another inspired by peanut butter and jelly sandwiches, which does double-duty as a great after-school snack.

Our Original Banana-Bread Baked Oatmeal

SERVES 6

Softened unsalted butter, for the baking dish

3 ripe medium bananas

2 cups old-fashioned rolled oats

2 cups milk of choice

¼ cup packed light brown sugar

1 large egg

2 tablespoons unsalted butter, melted

1 teaspoon vanilla extract

1 teaspoon baking powder

½ teaspoon ground cinnamon

½ teaspoon fine sea salt

¼ teaspoon ground nutmeg

½ cup dark chocolate chips

Chopped walnuts (optional), for serving

Maple syrup (optional), for serving

MAKE IT AHEAD

Prepare the oatmeal mixture the day before, cover it with plastic wrap, and refrigerate overnight. When ready to bake, follow the recipe as written.

Preheat the oven to 350°F. Grease a 7 × 11-inch baking dish (or five 4-inch ramekins [8 ounces each]) with butter and set aside.

In a large bowl, use a fork to mash the bananas until smooth. Add the oats, milk, brown sugar, egg, melted butter, vanilla, baking powder, cinnamon, salt, and nutmeg and whisk until thoroughly combined.

Pour the mixture into the prepared baking dish and sprinkle the top with the chocolate chips. Bake until the oatmeal is set and no longer loose in the center, 30 to 35 minutes (if using in ramekins, bake for 15 minutes).

Cut the oats into squares and serve with a sprinkle of walnuts and/or maple syrup, if desired.

Double-Chocolate Banana-Bread Baked Oatmeal

Make the batter as directed, adding ¼ cup unsweetened cocoa powder when adding the oats mixture. Bake as directed. To serve, omit the walnuts and sprinkle with slivered almonds, sweetened or unsweetened dried coconut flakes, and maple syrup.

Peanut Butter–Strawberry Banana-Bread Baked Oatmeal

Make the batter as directed, adding ¼ cup creamy peanut butter when adding the oats. Scrape into the pan. Omit the chocolate chips and sprinkle the top with 1 cup sliced (hulled) strawberries. Bake as directed. To serve, omit the walnuts and maple syrup and sprinkle with roughly chopped lightly salted peanuts and a dollop of strawberry preserves if you like.

Tips for Real Life

Store as grab-and-go single portions: After slicing the baked oatmeal, store individual portions in sealed containers in the refrigerator for up to 1 week or in the freezer for up to 3 months. Reheat in the microwave before serving.

For the peanut butter–strawberry variation, if raspberries look better (or are cheaper) at the store than strawberries, use them instead for sprinkling over the top and then serve with raspberry preserves.

Mama's Egyptian Falafel *(Ta'ameya)*
(recipe follows)

Mama's Egyptian Falafel *(Ta'ameya)*

In Egypt, falafel isn't something people typically make at home; instead, we get it from the nearest shop and grab a newspaper-bundled just-fried batch.

When our mom moved to the United States she was determined to figure out how to replicate that same authentic experience, which is how Egyptian falafel, or ta'ameya, became a standard feature of our weekend breakfast spread. Whether it was tucked into fresh warm pita and slathered with hummus and tahina sauce or heaped on a mezze platter with tomato and cucumber salad, hard-boiled eggs, a selection of cheeses, and tabbouleh, these perfectly crispy-yet-light balls were always the first thing to disappear.

Unlike most of its Mediterranean counterparts prepared with chickpeas, ta'ameya is made using only fava beans, plus tons of fresh cilantro and parsley. Favas are much lighter than chickpeas, and these fry up with distinctively fluffy and bright herby-green insides. Be sure to leave yourself time to soak the fava beans the night before.

SERVES 6 (MAKES 20 FALAFEL)

FALAFEL

2 cups dried split fava beans (our favorite is the Ziyad brand)

2 cups roughly chopped green onions, both white and green parts (about 2 bunches)

1 cup packed fresh cilantro leaves

1 small yellow onion, roughly chopped

4 medium garlic cloves, peeled but whole

1 tablespoon ground cumin

1 tablespoon ground coriander

1 tablespoon fine sea salt

2 teaspoons freshly ground black pepper

1 teaspoon baking powder

½ teaspoon baking soda

Vegetable oil, for frying

½ cup sesame seeds

FOR SERVING

Silky-Smooth Hummus (optional; page 94)

Baba's Tahina Sauce (optional; page 98)

Sliced veggies, such as tomatoes, bell peppers, radishes, lettuce, green onions, pickled cucumbers, and pickled turnips

MAKE THE FALAFEL: Soak the beans overnight at room temperature. Drain, rinse with cold water, and drain again.

In a food processor, combine the drained fava beans, green onions, cilantro, yellow onion, and garlic. Add 2 tablespoons water and process for 10 minutes. (Yes, this seems like a long time, but you want to ensure that the mixture is very, very smooth.) If you only have a small food processor, you can do this in batches.

Transfer the mixture to a large bowl and add the cumin, coriander, salt, pepper, baking powder, and baking soda. Mix thoroughly, then allow the mixture to rest at room temperature for 15 to 20 minutes, which will help the flavors meld and the texture to firm up slightly.

Line a plate with paper towels and place near the stove. Pour 3 inches oil into a large pot (pick one that is deep enough that the oil doesn't come any higher than halfway). Heat the oil over medium heat to about 350°F. (You'll know it's ready when you toss in a pinch of the fava mixture and it immediately sizzles but doesn't burn.)

While the oil is heating, shape the falafel mixture into ¼-cup-sized balls. Coat your hands with a little water or oil to keep the mixture from sticking. Sprinkle 1 teaspoon of the sesame seeds over each falafel ball.

Working in batches of 6 to 8 balls at a time (so you don't reduce the temperature of the oil, which leads to less crispy falafel), fry the falafel until they are golden brown and crispy all over, turning them as needed, 3 to 4 minutes total. Use a slotted spoon to transfer the falafel to the paper towels to drain.

TO SERVE: Enjoy hot with your favorite accompaniments. Our favorite combo is the falafel with tomatoes, cucumbers, and tahina sauce.

Store leftovers in an airtight container in the refrigerator for up to 5 days. Reheat until crispy and warmed through, 2 to 3 minutes in an air fryer at 350°F or 5 minutes in a 350°F oven.

Tip for Real Life

To make falafel that much easier, store some of the ta'ameya "dough" in the freezer. Simply prepare the base recipe as directed, excluding the baking powder, baking soda, cumin, coriander, salt, and pepper. Add the mixture to a large zip-top bag, flatten it to squeeze out as much air as possible, and freeze for up to 4 months. When ready to cook, thaw the mixture in the refrigerator overnight, stir in the remaining ingredients, and fry!

Middle Eastern Cottage Cheese Salad

As much as we love pancakes and French toast, savory breakfasts will always just feel right to us. In most Egyptian households, there really is no such thing as a "breakfast food," as in, we eat a lot of savory dishes in the morning that could just as easily work for lunch or dinner. So when we wanted to think up a fresh new take on a high-protein cottage cheese breakfast dish, our minds went to a savory salad. We loaded up the cool, tangy cheese with a Mediterranean-style mix of tomatoes, cucumbers, and olives, plus a creamy cumin-scented dressing. Topped with hard-boiled egg and avocado, it's the kind of dish that keeps you fueled up until your next meal. We like it scooped onto a piece of whole-grain bread, but it would also be great stuffed into a pita or lettuce cups.

MAKES 3 CUPS (SERVES 4)

1 pound whole-milk cottage cheese
(our favorite is Good Culture)

4 large eggs

TAHINI DRESSING

2 tablespoons well-stirred tahini

1 tablespoon fresh lime juice

1 teaspoon dried oregano

½ teaspoon distilled white vinegar

½ teaspoon ground cumin

½ teaspoon fine sea salt

½ teaspoon freshly ground black pepper

SALAD

1 medium Persian cucumber or ¼ English cucumber, finely chopped

1 large tomato on the vine or Roma tomato, seeded and diced

¼ cup pitted and finely chopped Kalamata olives

1 medium avocado, diced, for serving

Whole-grain bread, pita, or romaine lettuce wedges, for serving

Spoon the cottage cheese into a fine-mesh sieve and let drain for about 15 minutes, until no or very little liquid remains—it should look like a coarse ricotta cheese.

Meanwhile, bring a medium pot of water to a boil over medium-high heat. Add the eggs and cook for 9 minutes. Immediately drain the eggs and run them under cold water until cool to the touch. Peel, chop, and set aside.

MAKE THE TAHINI DRESSING: In a medium bowl or screw-top jar, combine the tahini, lime juice, oregano, vinegar, cumin, salt, and pepper. Add ¼ cup water and whisk or shake the dressing until smooth to combine well.

ASSEMBLE THE SALAD: In a large bowl, combine the drained cottage cheese, cucumber, tomato, and olives. Drizzle the dressing on top and give everything a gentle toss to coat. Top with the chopped egg and avocado. Serve with bread or lettuce, as desired.

MAKE IT AHEAD

To meal-prep this dish, chop the veggies up to 3 days ahead (store in an airtight container in the fridge), make the dressing up to 5 days ahead, and cook the hard-boiled eggs up to 1 week ahead (peel just before serving).

Tips for Real Life

You can use a lower-fat cottage cheese, if you prefer, but don't use anything less than 2% milk fat or it will change the consistency of the dish.

This recipe can easily be halved for fewer servings.

Coconut Chia Pudding Three Ways

When developing new recipes, our goal is pretty much figuring out how we can eat dessert for every meal. So when we got on the creamy, sweet chia pudding bandwagon, we knew that it would forever be a part of our morning menu rotation. In addition to being packed with protein and fiber and completely dairy-free, chia pudding is a personal favorite because you can flavor it up to suit your mood. Whether it's tropical mango, berries and crème, or apple-cinnamon and walnut, these three versions are guaranteed to be a welcome sight in your refrigerator when you want to grab a (morning or anytime) sweet treat.

Mango-Coconut Chia Pudding

SERVES 2

¼ cup chia seeds

½ cup unsweetened almond milk

½ cup canned light coconut milk

2 tablespoons maple syrup

1 teaspoon vanilla extract

¼ cup vanilla or plain yogurt, for serving

½ cup diced mango, for serving

Unsweetened coconut flakes (optional), for serving

In a medium bowl, combine the chia seeds, almond milk, coconut milk, maple syrup, and vanilla. Stir vigorously for a minute or two to evenly distribute the chia seeds.

Cover the bowl with plastic wrap or a lid and refrigerate for at least 4 hours or ideally overnight. You want the chia seeds to fully absorb the liquid, which will create a thick, creamy pudding-like texture.

To serve, give the pudding a good stir to break up any clumps. Divide the pudding between serving bowls or glasses, dollop with the yogurt, and top with the mango. Finish with a sprinkle of coconut flakes, if desired.

Tips for Real Life

You can use dairy or nondairy milk (almond, coconut, oat, or soy all work). Note that each type will lend a different flavor and texture to the pudding.

You can swap out the maple syrup for honey, agave, or even 1 small mashed ripe banana. If using honey or agave, start with a small amount and add more to taste.

Be sure to stir very well when you first combine the chia seeds and milk. This will help prevent clumping and ensure a nice, smooth pudding.

Get creative: Any of these puddings would be delicious topped with fresh fruit, nuts, seeds, granola, coconut flakes, or a spoonful of nut butter.

Strawberries and Crème Chia Pudding

Stir ½ cup diced (hulled) strawberries into the chia mixture. Serve dolloped with the yogurt and more chopped strawberries instead of mango. If desired, swap out the coconut for a spoonful of strawberry jam.

Apple-Coconut Chia Pudding with Cinnamon and Walnuts

Finely dice ½ apple such as Honeycrisp, Fuji, or Gala (we don't even bother to peel it). Stir the diced apple into the chia mixture. Dollop with the yogurt and instead of topping with mango and coconut, top with a dash of cinnamon, toasted walnuts, and raisins.

Lemon Ricotta Pancakes

There was a distinct time in our lives when we would beg for an "American" breakfast: pancakes or waffles, hash browns, OJ, the whole deal. But truth be told, once the initial novelty wore off, we couldn't help but feel like some of these morning standards were a little . . . one-note (sorry!). Compared to the spiced, herbed, saucy deliciousness we were treated to every morning, a stack of plain ol' pancakes just didn't, well, stack up. But we also know there's no breakfast that kids get more excited about than pancakes, so we decided to offer our take on the classic flapjack. With bright citrus and creamy, tangy ricotta, these thick, fluffy pancakes have really earned the center spot on the table.

MAKES 8 TO 10 PANCAKES (SERVES 4)

½ cup whole milk

Grated zest and juice of 1 large lemon (about 3 tablespoons)

1¼ cups all-purpose flour

3 tablespoons sugar

1½ teaspoons baking powder

½ teaspoon baking soda

½ teaspoon fine sea salt

3 large eggs

⅔ cup whole-milk ricotta cheese

3 tablespoons unsalted butter, melted, plus more for cooking and serving

1½ teaspoons vanilla extract

Maple syrup (optional), for serving

Fresh berries (optional), for serving

In a large bowl, combine the milk and lemon juice. Allow the mixture to sit at room temperature for 10 minutes to curdle slightly.

Meanwhile, in a medium bowl, whisk together the flour, sugar, baking powder, baking soda, and salt.

When the milk mixture is ready, whisk in the lemon zest, eggs, ricotta, melted butter, and vanilla. Gradually add the flour mixture, gently stirring with a wooden spoon until there are no longer any visible traces of flour. Do not overmix or you'll end up with tough pancakes!

Heat a griddle, large nonstick pan, or cast-iron skillet over medium-low heat. Add about 1 tablespoon butter to generously grease the cooking surface. Spoon the batter by the ⅓ cupful onto the griddle or pan, leaving at least 1 inch between the pancakes.

Cook the pancakes until the edges turn golden brown and the tops begin to bubble, 2 to 3 minutes. Carefully flip the pancakes and cook for another 2 minutes, or until the second side is golden brown and the pancake is cooked through (you can press on the center to check—it should spring back). Transfer the pancakes to a plate and repeat with the remaining batter, adding more butter to the griddle or pan as needed.

If desired, serve with butter, maple syrup, and/or fresh berries.

Tip for Real Life

Have some fun by creating a pancake topping bar! The spread of toppings can include a variety of fresh berries, preserves, whipped cream, maple syrup, chopped nuts, coconut flakes, Nutella, nut butter, chocolate syrup, your favorite cereals—make it as classic or crazy as you want!

Oven-Baked Shakshuka

When we think of eggs for breakfast, our minds don't go to scrambled, sunny-side up, or omelet . . . no, we're immediately thinking of runny yolks oozing into a rich, smoky tomato sauce dotted with feta, all scooped up with pita. And that, friends, is shakshuka. But while this classic Middle Eastern dish is traditionally made on the stove, we're moving things to the oven because no one needs to babysit a pan while juggling the morning chaos. Just toss everything in a dish, crack a few eggs over the top, and let the heat work its magic.

SERVES 4

2 cups cherry tomatoes, halved

1 large yellow onion, finely chopped

½ cup roughly chopped jarred roasted red peppers

3 tablespoons extra-virgin olive oil

1 small jalapeño pepper (optional), stemmed, seeded, and finely chopped (leave the seeds in if you want more heat)

4 medium garlic cloves, grated

1 teaspoon ground cumin

1 teaspoon smoked paprika

¾ teaspoon fine sea salt

¼ teaspoon cayenne pepper

¼ teaspoon Aleppo pepper or red pepper flakes

¼ teaspoon freshly ground black pepper

6 large eggs

FOR SERVING

Avocado slices

Crumbled brine-packed feta cheese

Chopped fresh cilantro

Pitas

Preheat the oven to 400°F.

In a 7 × 11-inch baking dish, combine the tomatoes, onion, roasted peppers, olive oil, jalapeño (if using), garlic, cumin, smoked paprika, salt, cayenne, Aleppo, and black pepper. Give everything a good toss to mix well and ensure the spices are evenly distributed.

Bake until the tomatoes have burst, about 40 minutes.

Carefully remove the dish from the oven, give everything a gentle stir, and create 6 wells in the tomato mixture. Crack an egg into each well, taking care not to break the yolk. Return the dish to the oven and bake until the whites are set but the yolks are still soft (you want them to be runny), 8 to 10 minutes.

TO SERVE: Top the shakshuka with avocado slices and crumbled feta and sprinkle with some cilantro. Serve with pita bread.

Store leftovers in an airtight container in the refrigerator for up to 3 days.

Tip for Real Life

Use any leftover sauce as a spread on toasted bread, a pasta sauce, or a topping for tomorrow morning's eggs.

Strawberry-Mascarpone Stuffed-Croissant French Toast

This is another great example of us not being able to simply leave things be. French toast is sweet and delicious! Everyone loves it! But we couldn't help but think we could do it better. Case in point: stuffing day-old croissants with a strawberry-studded ricotta/mascarpone blend and letting them luxuriate in custard before baking the whole thing (no greasy pan or flipping required). It tastes like the most expensive patisserie confection and yet it doesn't require spending a small fortune or a trip to the bakery. Prep this the night before you want to serve it, and simply pop it into the oven in the morning.

SERVES 6 TO 8

Softened unsalted butter, for the baking dish

4 large eggs

1 cup whole milk

2 teaspoons vanilla extract

½ teaspoon ground cinnamon

8 ounces mascarpone cheese, at room temperature

½ cup whole-milk ricotta cheese, at room temperature

½ cup granulated sugar

1 cup thinly sliced hulled strawberries

6 large stale croissants, halved horizontally

Powdered sugar or maple syrup (optional), for serving

Grease a 7 × 11-inch baking dish with butter and set aside.

In a medium bowl, whisk together the eggs, milk, 1 teaspoon of the vanilla, and the cinnamon until well combined. Set the custard aside.

In another medium bowl, stir together the mascarpone, ricotta, granulated sugar, and remaining 1 teaspoon vanilla. Gently fold in the strawberries.

Spread about ¼ cup of the mascarpone/strawberry mixture over the bottom half of each croissant. Add the top half over the filling and use a serrated knife to carefully slice each croissant vertically into 2-inch pieces.

Arrange the croissant slices cut-side up and staggered in the prepared baking dish and pour the custard over the top, making sure the croissants are evenly soaked. Cover the dish with plastic wrap and refrigerate for at least 4 hours or up to overnight.

Preheat the oven to 350°F.

Bake the croissant French toast until the top is golden brown and the custard is set, 35 to 40 minutes.

Let the French toast cool slightly before serving, either dusted with powdered sugar or drizzled with maple syrup, if desired.

Tips for Real Life

If you don't have day-old croissants, you can buy a fresh bag from the grocery store. Remove them from the package, place them on a sheet pan or plate, and leave them out, uncovered, overnight. Some bakeries will also sell you their day-olds at a discount.

Switch up the type of berries you use—raspberries and blueberries, or a mix, are all delicious.

Turkish Eggs with Za'atar Butter Sauce *(Çilbir)*

When we think of our favorite morning comfort-food dishes, this one is at the top of the list. It doesn't involve more than poaching a few eggs (fancy for "gently simmer in water for a few minutes"), sliding them onto a bed of garlicky yogurt, and drizzling them with a simple buttery, olive oil-y spice-infused sauce. It's the definition of elegant simplicity and yet it tastes like the kind of dish you need to go to culinary school to make.

SERVES 2 (BUT WE WON'T JUDGE IF IT'S FOR 1)

GARLICKY YOGURT

1 cup plain Greek yogurt, preferably whole-milk, at room temperature

1 or 2 medium garlic cloves (depending on how much garlic you like), finely minced

½ teaspoon fine sea salt

POACHED EGGS

2 large eggs

1 tablespoon distilled white vinegar

ZA'ATAR BUTTER SAUCE

2 tablespoons extra-virgin olive oil

2 tablespoons unsalted butter

2 teaspoons za'atar

1 teaspoon Aleppo pepper or red pepper flakes

1 teaspoon ground sumac

FOR SERVING

Fresh dill, roughly chopped

Pita or your favorite bread

MAKE THE GARLICKY YOGURT: In a small bowl, whisk together the yogurt, garlic, and salt until well blended. Divide the mixture between two serving bowls and set aside.

POACH THE EGGS: Fill a medium pot with about 4 cups water and bring to a boil over medium-high heat. Line a plate with a paper towel.

While the water comes to a boil, stir in the vinegar. Set a fine-mesh sieve over a small bowl. Crack the first egg into the sieve and allow any thin liquid to drain. (This will result in a neater-looking poached egg.)

Use a wooden spoon to gently swirl the water to create a whirlpool. Quickly slide the egg into the middle of the whirlpool and poach until the white is set, 2 to 3 minutes. Use a slotted spoon to transfer the egg to the paper towel to drain. Repeat with the remaining egg.

MAKE THE ZA'ATAR BUTTER SAUCE: In a medium saucepan, heat the olive oil and butter over medium-high heat. When the butter begins to foam, add the za'atar, Aleppo, and sumac. Stir to combine, then immediately remove the pan from the heat. Allow the spices to sit for at least 1 minute to allow the flavors to meld, but no more than a few minutes because you don't want them to cool too much.

TO SERVE: Top each bowl of yogurt with a poached egg, drizzle with the spiced butter sauce, and sprinkle with dill. Serve with pita or your favorite bread.

Tip for Real Life

Get creative: Beyond the basic components of this dish—eggs, yogurt, spiced butter—there's room for customization. Add some grated lemon or orange zest to the butter sauce for a citrusy punch, or some smoked paprika. Change up the type of yogurt you use, or add toppings like chopped fresh herbs, pepper flakes, or even toasted nuts.

Upside-Down Walnut & Honey Banana Bread

Like many households with kids, banana bread has been a staple recipe for us—namely because we always have very ripe (aka brown) bananas on the counter. We often turn them into banana bread, which also happens to be a fun and easy baking project (with kids or without), and also makes for a healthy breakfast and snack. Here we make the classic a little more exciting by using walnut and honey to create a crunchy, syrupy crust for this "upside-down" bread. It's your same beloved, dependable treat, just with a little more happening.

MAKES 8 THICK SLICES

Softened unsalted butter, for the loaf pan

HONEY-WALNUT TOPPING

5 tablespoons unsalted butter, melted

¼ cup packed light brown sugar

3 tablespoons honey

⅛ teaspoon fine sea salt

1 cup roughly chopped walnuts

BANANA BREAD

3 very ripe medium bananas

1 cup granulated sugar

8 tablespoons (1 stick/4 ounces) unsalted butter, melted

2 large eggs

2 teaspoons vanilla extract

½ cup whole-milk plain Greek yogurt

1 teaspoon baking soda

¾ teaspoon fine sea salt

1¾ cups all-purpose flour

½ teaspoon ground cinnamon

MAKE THE HONEY-WALNUT TOPPING: Preheat the oven to 350°F. Grease a 9 × 5-inch loaf pan with butter and line a sheet pan with foil or parchment paper.

In a medium bowl, stir together the melted butter, brown sugar, honey, and salt. Add the walnuts and stir until well coated. Evenly spread the walnut mixture over the bottom of the prepared loaf pan and set aside.

MAKE THE BANANA BREAD: In a medium bowl, use a fork to mash the bananas until smooth and creamy.

In a large bowl, whisk together the granulated sugar and melted butter. Add the eggs and vanilla and whisk until well combined. Add the mashed banana, yogurt, baking soda, and salt and whisk again to combine.

While stirring with a wooden spoon, gradually add the flour, followed by the cinnamon. Stir just until the batter reaches a smooth texture. Take care not to overmix or you'll end up with tough banana bread.

Pour the banana bread batter evenly over the walnut topping. Set the pan on top of the lined sheet pan to catch any drips.

Bake until a toothpick inserted into the center comes out clean, 1 hour to 1 hour 5 minutes. If the top begins to brown around the 45-minute mark, lightly tent the bread with foil and continue baking.

Let the bread cool in the pan on a rack for about 10 minutes, then invert it onto a plate and let cool completely. Slice and serve.

Store leftovers in an airtight container at room temperature for up to 2 days. Or wrap in plastic wrap and freeze for up to 3 months.

Tip for Real Life

We like to freeze our bananas once they've reached peak ripeness so we always have them handy—and we never have to throw any away (frozen bananas make the best smoothies!). Simply peel them and toss them into a freezer-safe container or zip-top bag and freeze for up to 1 month.

Spicy Tomato Scrambled Eggs

This is another dish that has often appeared on our weekend breakfast table. It can best be described as a mash-up of eggah, an Arab omelet packed with spices, and Turkish menamen, which is scrambled eggs with tomatoes, peppers, and onions. So translation: extra-delicious eggs that we've made even more decadent with a dash of smoky paprika, fresh cilantro, and classic gooey cheese-pull mozzarella. We'd typically enjoy this with stewed fava beans (ful) and feta and tomatoes (page 32), but you really don't need more than good pita to make it a perfect meal.

SERVES 4

1 tablespoon extra-virgin olive oil

½ medium red onion, finely diced

2 medium jalapeño peppers (optional), stemmed, seeded (or leave the seeds in if you want more heat), and finely diced

2 medium Roma tomatoes, seeded and diced

1 medium garlic clove, minced

¼ teaspoon fine sea salt, plus more to taste

¼ teaspoon freshly ground black pepper (optional)

⅛ teaspoon smoked paprika

8 large eggs, beaten

½ cup shredded low-moisture mozzarella cheese

⅓ cup finely chopped fresh cilantro leaves

1 tablespoon unsalted butter

In a large nonstick skillet, heat the olive oil over medium-high heat until it shimmers. Add the onion and jalapeños (if using), reduce the heat to medium, and cook, stirring occasionally, until the onion turns translucent and has not yet begun to brown, 3 to 4 minutes.

Use a silicone spatula to stir in the tomatoes, garlic, salt, pepper (if using), and smoked paprika and cook, stirring frequently, until the tomatoes soften and release some of their liquid, another 3 to 4 minutes.

Add the eggs and use the spatula to gently stir the mixture, bringing the ingredients from the edges of the pan to the middle. (A slow and delicate scrambling process will ensure soft, fluffy eggs!) After about 2 minutes, as the eggs just begin to set, add the mozzarella, cilantro, and butter. Continue gently stirring until the cheese is melted, about 1 minute. If you prefer firmer scrambled eggs, continue cooking until they reach your desired doneness. Serve hot.

MAKE IT AHEAD

You can meal-prep this dish and reduce your cook time by more than half. Precook the vegetables, allow them to cool, then store in an airtight container in the refrigerator for up to 5 days. When ready to finish the dish, return them to the pan and proceed with the recipe as directed.

Egyptian Fava Bean Salad *(Ful Medames with Tahini)*

Fava bean salad, known as "ful," holds a special place in the hearts of Egyptians. It's a dish that's usually an integral part of the weekend breakfast routine, and certainly has been for us for as long as we can remember. One of our favorite memories of visits to Egypt was of our aunt hurrying to the nearby shop to pick up fresh falafel and ful for us to enjoy in the morning. Ful continues to be a big part of our breakfast, brunch, and now "brinner" rotation (who doesn't love a hearty bowl of creamy mashed cumin- and lime-spiked fava beans at any time of the day?). The traditional method for making ful keeps things pretty simple and dip-like, but we've come to love a more salad-like approach with bits of tomatoes, bell peppers, and green onions. It's a true reflection of who we are and what we're about.

SERVES 4 TO 6

1 (15-ounce) can fava beans, drained and thoroughly rinsed

¼ cup well-stirred tahini

4 tablespoons extra-virgin olive oil

3 tablespoons fresh lime juice (1 to 2 large limes)

1 medium garlic clove, minced

1 teaspoon ground cumin

½ teaspoon sea salt

¼ teaspoon freshly ground black pepper

1½ medium Roma tomatoes, finely chopped (about ½ cup)

1 small green bell pepper, finely chopped (about ½ cup)

1 green onion, both white and green parts, finely chopped (about ¼ cup)

¼ cup chopped fresh flat-leaf Italian parsley leaves, plus more for garnish

Warm pitas, for serving

In a small saucepan, combine the fava beans and ¾ cup water. Bring to a boil over high heat. Reduce the heat to medium-high and cook the beans until the water reduces by half, 8 to 10 minutes.

Remove the pot from the heat and use a potato masher or the back of a fork to mash the beans (the fork will yield a more rustic, chunky mash if that's what you prefer).

Transfer the beans to a large bowl and stir in the tahini, 3 tablespoons of the olive oil, the lime juice, garlic, cumin, salt, and pepper until well combined. Fold in the tomatoes, bell pepper, green onion, and parsley until evenly distributed.

Drizzle the remaining 1 tablespoon of olive oil over the top and sprinkle with parsley. Serve with warm pita bread.

The salad is best enjoyed right away, but you could store leftovers in an airtight container in the refrigerator for up to 2 days.

Homemade Labneh & Smoked Salmon Dip

For this easy appetizer, we really did go Middle East meets Midwest. Tangy, creamy labneh—one of our favorite condiments that is so good dolloped on any sweet or savory dish—gets layered with the best elements of a bagel brunch, including smoked salmon, capers, and fresh dill. Yes, it takes time for the yogurt to drain and transform into the thickest, richest version of itself (labneh!), but otherwise, this is almost completely hands-off. And once you have a batch of labneh in the fridge, this fresh, sophisticated-feeling starter, snack, or light lunch comes together in minutes.

SERVES 4

1½ cups Labneh (page 91)

6 ounces smoked salmon

1 medium Persian cucumber, thinly sliced or chopped

½ cup halved cherry tomatoes

¼ cup sliced pitted Kalamata olives

2 tablespoons brine-packed capers, drained

3 tablespoons extra-virgin olive oil

1 tablespoon za'atar

Finely chopped fresh dill, for garnish

Finely chopped fresh chives, for garnish

Homemade Pita Chips (page 85), pita bread, baguette, ciabatta, or bagels, for serving

Make the labneh as directed. Note that you have to start this at least the night before you want to serve this.

Spread the labneh over a plate and top with the smoked salmon, cucumbers, tomatoes, olives, and capers. Drizzle with the olive oil and finish with the za'atar. Garnish with a sprinkle of dill and chives and serve with chips or bread for dipping or schmearing.

Just Getting Started

Here at Food Dolls HQ, we have perfected a new sport: grazing. It's a little more substantial than snacking but not quite the same as having a full meal, and it always calls for something you can tear into with your hands, whether you're smearing and scooping or popping until you can't stop(ping). Call it girl dinner. Call it all-day snacks. But ultimately, these are the dishes that we're reaching for when we want something to take the edge off and are not about to settle for a basic bag of chips (even though these recipes are nearly as easy as ripping open a bag!). The recipes in this chapter deliver much bigger, better results in the flavor and presentation department. They are your quick and easy starters that you can serve before dinner, as party apps, or need-something-now eats. No matter what you call them, they're delicious.

Turkey Burger Sliders with Salatit Zabadi

It's hard to improve on a smoky, juicy burger tucked inside a sweet, doughy bun and slathered in sauce. Oh wait, we did! We swapped out the beef for leaner turkey, which when flavored with parsley, paprika, and sun-dried tomatoes (all chopped in the food processor to keep things extra quick), takes on a rich, deep flavor. We made them slider-sized so you can cook them more quickly and eat them sooner—but also so they can be easily served as part of a party spread, be tucked into school lunches, or act as kid-friendly servings at dinner. But what really puts these over the top is a drizzle of creamy, tangy salatit zabadi, or cucumber yogurt salad, which gives you that necessary dribble-down-the-chin effect. Whether you make these on the grill, on the stove, in the oven, or in an air-fryer (yes you can! see Tips), you'll be able to have a slider moment in less than 30 minutes.

MAKES 12 SLIDERS

Extra-virgin olive oil or cooking spray (optional), for the sheet pan

¾ cup packed fresh flat-leaf parsley leaves

½ small red onion, roughly chopped

¼ cup oil-packed sun-dried tomatoes, drained

1 medium garlic clove, peeled but whole

2 pounds ground turkey (93/7)

1 teaspoon smoked paprika

1 teaspoon fine sea salt

½ teaspoon dried oregano

½ teaspoon freshly ground black pepper

ASSEMBLY

12 small slider buns, preferably brioche

Baby arugula

3 medium Roma tomatoes, sliced

Salatit Zabadi (page 101)

Sumac Onions (page 102) or thinly sliced yellow onion

Spicy Zhoug Sauce (optional; page 88)

Preheat the oven to 375°F. Line a sheet pan with parchment paper or lightly grease with olive oil or cooking spray.

In a food processor, combine the parsley, onion, sun-dried tomatoes, and garlic. Pulse until the mixture is roughly chopped.

In a medium bowl, combine the ground turkey, the parsley mixture, smoked paprika, salt, oregano, and pepper. Mix just until combined. (Overmixing will yield tough/dense burgers.) Form the mixture into 12 patties (roughly ⅓ cup each).

Arrange the patties on the prepared sheet pan, leaving room between them. Bake until the juices run clear and an instant-read thermometer inserted in the center registers 165°F, 20 to 25 minutes, flipping halfway through.

TO ASSEMBLE: Lay a patty on the bottom half of each bun. Top with a handful of arugula and some tomato slices. Slather the top bun with the salatit zabadi, heap with sumac onions, and place it on top. Serve with zhoug, if desired.

Tips for Real Life

Air-fry it: Preheat an air fryer to 380°F and add the patties to the air fryer basket in a single layer (working in batches, if necessary). Air-fry for 15 to 18 minutes, flipping halfway through, or until an instant-read thermometer inserted in the center registers 165°F.

Make it on the stovetop: Heat a tablespoon of olive oil in a large skillet or grill pan over medium heat. When the oil shimmers, add the patties and cook until both sides are browned and the center has a temperature of 165°F, about 4 minutes per side.

For full-size burgers, form the turkey mixture into 6 patties about ⅔ cup each. Cook them for closer to 12 minutes if grilling, 20 to 25 minutes if baking, or 20 to 22 minutes if air-frying.

Sumac Chicken Wings

With the sunny pop of sumac and lemon, spices like oregano and paprika, and a lighter feel thanks to baking (or air-frying, see Tips), these wings taste like they just came home from a summer abroad. We like to serve them with a side of Greek yogurt or salatit zabadi for dunking.

SERVES 4

Extra-virgin olive oil, as needed

1½ pounds chicken wingettes (flats) and drumettes

2 teaspoons ground sumac

1 teaspoon ground cumin

1 teaspoon fine sea salt

1 teaspoon smoked paprika

1 teaspoon onion powder

1 teaspoon dried oregano

1 teaspoon garlic powder

½ teaspoon cayenne pepper (optional; or use less if you don't like spice)

1 tablespoon fresh lemon juice

⅓ cup loosely packed fresh flat-leaf parsley leaves

Flaky sea salt, to taste

Greek yogurt or Salatit Zabadi (page 101), for serving (optional)

Preheat the oven to 400°F. Line a sheet pan with foil or parchment paper and set a wire rack on top. (This is optional, but it will help keep the wings crispy.) Brush the rack with a little oil to keep the chicken from sticking.

Thoroughly pat dry the chicken with paper towels. (This will help the spice blend adhere to the skin and will ensure the wings get extra crispy.) In a large bowl, stir together the sumac, cumin, salt, smoked paprika, onion powder, oregano, garlic powder, and cayenne (if using). Add the chicken and toss well to ensure all the pieces are evenly coated. (Your hands work really well for this.)

Arrange the wings on the rack and bake until they are deeply browned and crispy and the juices run clear, 45 minutes to 1 hour, flipping halfway through.

Immediately drizzle the wings with the lemon juice and top with the parsley and sprinkle of flaky sea salt. Enjoy hot with yogurt or sauce for dipping, if desired.

Tips for Real Life

If you don't want to get your hands all up in the chicken and spice mix, you can add the spices and chicken to a large resealable plastic bag and give everything a good shake to coat.

Air-fry it: Spray an air fryer basket with cooking spray and preheat the air fryer to 380°F. Arrange the wings in the basket in a single layer (working in batches, if necessary) and air-fry for 28 minutes, flipping halfway through.

Grill it: Preheat the grill to medium-high and coat the grates with oil. Grill, turning occasionally, until the wings are crispy and the juices run clear, 25 to 30 minutes.

Don't be tempted to use bottled lemon juice—there's no substitute for the bright pop of flavor that fresh provides.

No-Knead Za'atar Focaccia (recipe follows)

No-Knead Za'atar Focaccia

Can we tell you a secret? Even though we've been cooking for a living for more than eight years, we've always been intimidated by baking bread. Between dealing with the gloopy dough, the resting, and the mysterious magic that happens in the oven, it's always just felt like a bit . . . much. So when we heard about an easier than easy no-knead recipe for focaccia, we knew we needed to give it a shot. And when we pulled that first perfectly tender loaf out of the oven, we realized not only what a game-changer this recipe was, but also how similar to a popular Middle Eastern bread called manakeesh it is. Manakeesh is also fluffy and olive oil-y, plus it's loaded with earthy za'atar seasoning. So we're combining the best of both worlds and gifting you with a flavorful, foolproof recipe that could actually turn you into the kind of person who puts fresh-baked bread on the table for dinner. (Just be sure to figure in enough time for your dough to rest, which can be done a few days ahead of time.) We love this alongside pasta, soups, and salads; as part of a cheese or charcuterie board; or sliced horizontally and used as sandwich bread.

MAKES ONE 9 × 13-INCH FOCACCIA
(SERVES 8 TO 10)

4 cups all-purpose or bread flour
(see Tips), plus more as needed

2 teaspoons instant yeast

2 teaspoons fine sea salt

1 teaspoon sugar

2 cups lukewarm water

4 tablespoons extra-virgin olive oil

Unsalted butter or cooking spray
(optional), for greasing

3 tablespoons za'atar

1 teaspoon flaky sea salt

In a large bowl, whisk together the flour, yeast, fine sea salt, and sugar. Add the lukewarm water and mix with a rubber spatula until the liquid is absorbed and the mixture forms a sticky ball.

Drizzle 1 tablespoon of the olive oil over the dough and cover the bowl with a damp tea towel or plastic wrap. Refrigerate for at least 12 hours or up to 3 days.

Line a deep 9 × 13-inch pan with parchment paper or lightly grease with butter or cooking spray. Drizzle 2 tablespoons of the olive oil in the center of the pan.

Using your hands, very gently deflate the dough by releasing it from the sides of the bowl and pulling it toward the center, forming a rough ball. (You want to use a light hand here to preserve the air pockets that develop during fermentation; that's what makes for a light, airy loaf!) Place the dough ball on top of the olive oil in the pan and roll it around to evenly coat the outside. Let the dough rest at room temperature for 3 to 4 hours, until doubled in size. The dough should slowly fill in when dented with your finger. If it bounces back right away, it needs more time.

Preheat the oven to 425°F.

Pour the remaining 1 tablespoon olive oil over the dough and use all of your fingers to create deep dimples all over the dough, down to the bottom of the pan. (This helps give the bread that signature focaccia texture.) As you do this, you also want to be gently spreading the dough so it fills the entire pan. The dough should be wet and sticky, but if it's unmanageable, you can add more flour, 1 tablespoon at a time, folding the dough over the additional flour and gently pressing to incorporate, until it's not a nightmare to work with.

Sprinkle the dough with the za'atar and flaky salt.

Bake until the top of the bread is golden and crisp, 25 to 30 minutes.

Let the focaccia cool in the pan on a wire rack for at least 10 minutes before slicing and serving.

Focaccia is best enjoyed fresh, but if you have leftovers, you can store them in an airtight container at room temperature for up to 2 days. Gently reheat it in the oven or toaster to refresh the texture.

Tips for Real Life

Both all-purpose and bread flour will work for this recipe. We love all-purpose because we always have it in the pantry, but bread flour will give your focaccia a chewier texture because of its higher protein content.

Get creative: Change the toppings that you use. Sun-dried tomatoes, olives, fresh herbs, and sesame seeds would all be super tasty.

We recommend using a sharp serrated knife when slicing the focaccia so you don't end up pressing or smooshing the bread too much.

Olive Cheese Bread

Whether you've been following us on social for years or are just getting to know us now, you can tell that we like to keep things simple (at least when it comes to food). This go-to starter-snack is no different, but we don't consider it to be simple because of how easy the recipe is to make (although it is), but because of how little work we need to do to convince you to make it. Blend three kinds of cheese with chopped olives and roasted red peppers, slather it over good crusty bread, and bake until bubbling, ooey, and gooey—there isn't anything more to say than that. Well, except that you could also make it a meal with a light salad or bowl of soup.

SERVES 12

1 cup shredded low-moisture mozzarella cheese

¾ cup freshly grated parmesan cheese

8 tablespoons (1 stick/4 ounces) unsalted butter, at room temperature

4 ounces cream cheese

½ cup pitted Manzanilla olives, roughly chopped

½ cup pitted Kalamata olives, roughly chopped

3 green onions, both white and green parts, finely chopped

¼ cup finely chopped jarred roasted red peppers

½ teaspoon freshly ground black pepper

Pinch of Aleppo pepper or red pepper flakes (optional)

1 (1-pound) loaf French bread

Finely chopped fresh flat-leaf parsley or basil leaves (optional), for serving

MAKE IT AHEAD

The cheese mixture can be stored in an airtight container in the refrigerator for up to 3 days. Let it come to room temperature (about 45 minutes out of the fridge) before spreading it over the bread.

Preheat the oven to 350°F.

In a large bowl, stir together the mozzarella, parm, butter, cream cheese, both olives, the green onions, roasted peppers, black pepper, and Aleppo (if using) until well combined.

Slice the bread through the middle horizontally. Divide the cheese mixture between the halves and spread it so it completely covers the surface of each half of bread.

Set the bread cheese-side up on a sheet pan or in an ovenproof dish and bake until the cheese has melted and the top is beginning to brown, 20 to 25 minutes. If you want an even bubblier golden crust (completely optional, but worth it), you could switch to broil for the final 1 to 2 minutes of baking.

Let the bread cool slightly before cutting into 2-inch-wide slices and serving warm. Sprinkle with herbs, if desired.

Leftovers can be stored in an airtight container in the refrigerator for up to 3 days. To reheat, wrap the bread in foil and heat in the oven at 350°F until warm and gooey again, 8 to 10 minutes.

Tips for Real Life

Using different types of olives is one way to change up the flavor of this bread. You can try buttery Castelvetrano or classic pizzeria-style canned black olives.

Different cheeses will also give this a different personality. Stick with varieties that melt well (like your cheddars and your Jacks) and go for a blend of sharp and mild.

If you don't have jarred roasted peppers in your pantry, you could make this with an equal amount of sun-dried tomatoes or finely chopped fresh red bell peppers.

If you're a fan of fresh herbs, consider adding 2 teaspoons of finely chopped rosemary or thyme for even more depth of flavor.

You could also ditch the bread and serve the warm cheese filling as a dip with pita chips or as a sandwich spread. Bake the cheese in an 8- to 10-inch round heatproof dish or skillet in the oven at 350°F until the top is golden and bubbling, 15 to 20 minutes.

Crispy Baked Halloumi with Hot Honey Drizzle

Halloumi is a firm, salty cheese that comes from Cyprus but pops up all over Mediterranean cooking. We especially love it for its punchy flavor, plus the way it manages to soften but not totally dissolve. When cubed, dredged with spiced bread crumbs, and pan-fried, it transforms into something that's a much more interesting mozzarella stick, especially when drizzled with hot honey. You could serve this on its own as an appetizer—with a tangy dip like Red Pepper Walnut Dip (page 95) or Spicy Zhoug Sauce (page 88)—or scatter the Halloumi cubes over a salad, but either way, it's a sophisticated touch that no one would ever guess is this simple to make.

MAKES 12 PIECES

Extra-virgin olive oil or neutral oil, as needed

1 large egg

¾ cup panko bread crumbs

1 teaspoon garlic powder

1 teaspoon Italian seasoning

1 teaspoon smoked paprika

½ teaspoon freshly ground black pepper

¼ teaspoon fine sea salt

8 ounces Halloumi cheese, cut into 1-inch cubes

2 tablespoons honey

2 teaspoons Aleppo pepper or red pepper flakes

Preheat the oven to 400°F. Line a sheet pan with foil or parchment paper and lightly coat with olive oil. Set aside.

In a small bowl, use a fork to beat the egg well. In a medium bowl, stir together the panko, garlic powder, Italian seasoning, smoked paprika, black pepper, and salt.

Dip each cube of Halloumi into the egg and allow any excess to drip off before tossing in the panko mixture. Make sure the cubes are coated completely and evenly on all sides, gently pressing the panko to help it stick.

Arrange the dredged Halloumi in a single layer on the prepared sheet pan, making sure that none of the cubes are touching. (This will ensure that they get nice and crispy.) Drizzle more olive oil over the Halloumi so all of the cubes are evenly coated (your second guarantee for crisp Halloumi).

Bake until the Halloumi is golden, 14 to 16 minutes, gently flipping the cubes about halfway through.

While the Halloumi bakes, in a small bowl, stir together the honey and Aleppo.

Immediately transfer the finished Halloumi to a serving platter and drizzle with the hot honey. Serve hot and gooey.

MAKE IT AHEAD

Coat the Halloumi in the panko, arrange the cubes on the sheet pan, and cover with plastic wrap. Store in the freezer for up to 2 months. (We don't recommend doing this in the refrigerator because the panko coating will get soggy.) To bake, either thaw and bake as directed or bake from frozen and add 8 to 10 minutes to the cook time. You can also assemble the hot honey and store it in an airtight container in the refrigerator for up to 2 weeks. Give it a good stir before drizzling it over the Halloumi.

Tips for Real Life

When cutting the Halloumi into cubes, do your best to make them as uniform as possible, which will help them cook evenly.

For a gluten-free option, you can use gluten-free panko bread crumbs.

For extra, extra crispy Halloumi, add 1 tablespoon freshly grated parmesan to the panko mixture.

Air-fry it: Arrange the Halloumi in a single layer in an air fryer basket (working in batches, if necessary) and air-fry at 400°F for about 10 minutes, flipping them halfway through.

Spicy Honey-Harissa Cauliflower Bites

These crispy-creamy bites are all you're going to be thinking about for your next party. We dredge florets in a panko breading, roast them until golden, and then drape them in a sweet-salty-spicy harissa honey with heaps of fresh cilantro. The result? Dreamy, extremely craveable, and even (dare we say) healthy cauliflower. Try them served over rice as a main dish!

SERVES 4

CAULIFLOWER BITES

Extra-virgin olive oil, as needed

2 large eggs

2 cups panko bread crumbs

1 small head cauliflower (about 12 ounces)

SPICY HARISSA HONEY

2 teaspoons cornstarch

¼ cup honey

2 tablespoons harissa

2 tablespoons reduced-sodium soy sauce

2 medium garlic cloves, minced

¼ teaspoon ground cumin

FOR SERVING

¼ cup finely chopped fresh cilantro leaves

1 tablespoon sesame seeds, toasted (see Dry-Toasting, page 29)

Tip for Real Life

Using precut cauliflower florets is an option, but just remember that it's ideal for the florets to all be roughly the same size. That said, you can look for a bag with relatively uniform florets or trim them that way.

MAKE THE CAULIFLOWER BITES: Preheat the oven to 400°F. Line a sheet pan with foil or parchment paper and brush to coat well with olive oil (about 2 tablespoons).

In a small bowl, use a fork to beat the eggs until well combined and uniform in color. Put the panko in a medium bowl. Set both aside.

Trim or tear off the leaves from the base of the cauliflower, then trim off the stem end. Starting from the center of the cauliflower, use your hands to break apart the florets. Ideally, all the florets will be similar in size, which will ensure that they cook at the same rate, so use a knife to trim down any larger florets. If any of your florets have thick stems, you can trim those, too. If your florets have any dirt or debris, you can rinse them under cold water and pat them dry with a clean kitchen towel.

Dip each floret into the egg, letting any excess drip off. Then roll the florets in the panko, pressing them with your hands to make sure they're well coated. Arrange the cauliflower in a single layer on the prepared sheet pan, leaving space between them, which will help them crisp up versus steam. Drizzle more olive oil over the top; just enough to lightly coat the cauliflower.

Roast the cauliflower until the florets are golden brown and fork-tender, 25 to 30 minutes, flipping about halfway through.

MEANWHILE, MAKE THE SPICY HARISSA HONEY: In a small bowl, stir the cornstarch with 1 tablespoon water.

In a medium saucepan, combine the honey, harissa, soy sauce, garlic, and cumin. Bring the mixture to a simmer, stirring occasionally, over medium heat. Stir in the cornstarch mixture and continue stirring until the sauce returns to a simmer and thickens, about 2 minutes. Transfer the sauce to a large bowl.

TO SERVE: Add the crispy cauliflower to the bowl with the sauce and gently toss to coat. Spoon the cauliflower into a serving bowl and sprinkle with the cilantro and sesame seeds. Serve warm.

Store leftovers in an airtight container in the refrigerator for up to 3 days.

Spinach & Cheese Pita Pockets

Who doesn't know and love a pita pocket? That said, we'll go so far as claiming that you haven't really pita'd (yes, we turned *pita* into a verb!) if you haven't had one stuffed with a molten, gooey spinach and cheese filling. It's essentially teaming up two of our favorite things, spinach dip and pita, then giving them even more of a Midwest/MidEast makeover by adding tangy feta and heaps of fresh herbs to the mix. All there is to do is stir, stuff, and bake and you have a no-brainer starter, lunch, after-school snack, or dinner that you could enjoy on its own or with salatit zabadi or hummus.

MAKES 8 PITA POCKETS

3 tablespoons extra-virgin olive oil, plus more for greasing

1 medium yellow onion, finely chopped

16 ounces baby spinach

2 medium garlic cloves, minced

1 cup shredded low-moisture mozzarella cheese

1 (4-ounce) block brine-packed feta cheese, crumbled

⅓ cup cream cheese, at room temperature

¼ cup finely chopped fresh dill

¼ cup finely chopped fresh cilantro leaves

¼ cup finely chopped fresh flat-leaf parsley leaves

2 green onions, both white and green parts, finely chopped

½ teaspoon fine sea salt

½ teaspoon freshly ground black pepper

4 (8-inch) pitas

Salatit Zabadi (page 101) or Silky-Smooth Hummus (page 94), for dipping (optional)

MAKE IT AHEAD

You can assemble the pockets up to 3 days in advance, wrap them in plastic wrap, and store them in the refrigerator. Bake as directed just before serving.

In a large skillet, heat the oil over medium-high heat until it shimmers. Add the yellow onion and sauté, stirring occasionally, until they are soft and translucent but not yet beginning to brown, 5 to 6 minutes.

Add the spinach and carefully stir to incorporate it with the onion. (Yes, it will look like a ton at first, but it will cook down; add a few handfuls at a time if your pan can't handle all of it at once.) Gently mix until the spinach is tender and bright green, 2 to 3 minutes. Add the garlic and cook until fragrant, about another minute. Transfer the mixture to a large bowl and allow it to cool to room temperature, about 30 minutes.

Preheat the oven to 350°F. Lightly coat a sheet pan with olive oil and set aside.

Once the spinach mixture has cooled, add the mozzarella, feta, cream cheese, dill, cilantro, parsley, green onions, salt, and pepper and mix until everything is well combined.

Carefully cut the pitas in half crosswise and gently open the pockets. Fill each pita pocket with about ⅓ cup of the spinach and cheese mixture. If any of your pitas tear, you can either patch the hole with a small piece of another pita or just ignore it—the filling will usually stay put once baked. Place the stuffed pitas on the prepared sheet pan and brush both sides of each pita with olive oil.

Bake until the filling is melted and bubbling and the pitas are golden, 14 to 16 minutes, flipping about halfway through. If you want to get a little more color on the pitas and filling, you could switch the oven to broil for the last 1 to 2 minutes of baking. (Just keep a close eye to avoid burning.)

Serve hot with dipping sauce, if desired.

Store any leftovers in an airtight container in the refrigerator for up to 3 days. Reheat them in an oven or toaster to maintain their crispness.

Tomato, Arugula & Ricotta Toasts

We learned early that a great salad doesn't need much more than sweet in-season tomatoes, some garlic, a little olive oil, and salt. This simple preparation was frequently on offer for any meal, any time of day, and we treated it just as much as a condiment as we did a salad. We wanted to really let this combination shine by turning it into a bite-sized toast, adorned with milky, creamy ricotta and spicy arugula. It's the kind of easy, breezy dish you throw together on a summer afternoon when you can't be bothered to turn on the stove, and everyone will be grateful you did. Serve these on their own, or add a side salad or bowl of soup to round out the meal.

SERVES 10 TO 12

1 (26-inch) baguette, cut into 1-inch slices

¼ cup extra-virgin olive oil, plus more for drizzling

4 cups (2 pounds) grape tomatoes, quartered

1 medium garlic clove, minced

½ teaspoon fine sea salt, plus more to taste

½ teaspoon freshly ground black pepper

1 cup whole-milk ricotta cheese

Baby arugula, for serving

Preheat the oven to 400°F.

Arrange the baguette slices on a sheet pan and drizzle both sides with olive oil.

Bake until the toasts are golden and crispy, about 15 minutes, flipping them halfway through. Allow them to cool slightly before assembling.

Meanwhile, in a medium bowl, combine the tomatoes, ¼ cup olive oil, the garlic, salt, and pepper and gently toss to combine.

Spread the ricotta over each toast and generously spoon the tomato mixture over the top. Finish with a tuft of arugula, a drizzle of oil, and a pinch of salt.

Serve immediately so your toasts don't get soggy.

Tips for Real Life

Using different-colored tomatoes, if you can find them, will make this otherwise simple dish even more visually appealing.

If arugula's peppery flavor is too strong for you, you can substitute it with a milder leafy green, such as basil, spinach, or mixed greens.

Goat cheese, cream cheese, or even a soft feta would be great in place of the ricotta.

For a touch of heat, add a pinch of Aleppo pepper or red pepper flakes to the tomato mixture.

A drizzle of balsamic glaze makes these feel even fancier with barely any extra effort. You could also add a sprinkle of toasted pine nuts.

Pizza "Pie"

We are all about a tasty mash-up, especially when it means making some of our favorite foods in a fraction of the time. Here we're inspired by an impossibly gooey three-cheese pizza topped with peppers and olives, but instead of using traditional pizza dough, we're layering everything up in buttery store-bought phyllo dough, spinach pie–style. It's the most delicious hack ever, especially when it's assembled as a fuss-free casserole. Slice this up for a fun weeknight meal alongside a salad, or serve this as a bite-sized nibble for a party.

SERVES 8 TO 16

1 pound frozen phyllo dough sheets (see Tips), thawed in the refrigerator overnight

¾ cup pitted Kalamata olives, finely chopped

Melted unsalted butter, for the baking dish

¼ cup pitted Manzanilla olives, finely chopped

10 tablespoons (1¼ sticks/5 ounces) unsalted butter, melted

2 cups finely chopped mixed bell peppers (about 3 small green, red, and orange/yellow peppers)

1 cup shredded low-moisture mozzarella cheese

½ cup shredded mild cheddar cheese

½ cup freshly grated parmesan cheese

1 tablespoon Italian seasoning

¾ cup whole milk

2 large eggs

½ teaspoon freshly ground black pepper

¼ teaspoon fine sea salt

MAKE IT AHEAD

You can assemble the pie right up until you soak it. Cover it tightly with plastic wrap and refrigerate it overnight (though no longer than that), then move ahead with soaking and baking.

Set the phyllo dough (still in the box) on the counter to come to room temperature for 1 hour before using. Pat the chopped olives dry with paper towels and set aside.

Brush the bottom of a 9 × 13-inch metal baking dish with butter, ensuring that it completely coats the surface.

Lay a sheet of the phyllo in the prepared baking dish and brush it with some of the melted butter. Keep the rest of the sheets covered with a towel so they don't dry out. Repeat this process, layering and brushing, until you have used half of the phyllo sheets.

Create a layer of the bell peppers, followed by the mozzarella, cheddar, and parm. Scatter both the olives over the cheese and sprinkle with the Italian seasoning.

Continue layering and buttering the phyllo over the filling, one sheet at a time, until you've run out of phyllo. At this point, slice the assembled pie into pieces, which will make it easier to serve. (We do 16 squares if serving this as an appetizer, 32 if going for smaller bites.)

In a medium bowl, whisk together the milk, eggs, black pepper, and salt until well combined. Pour the mixture evenly over the pie and allow the pie to sit and soak for 20 minutes.

Meanwhile, preheat the oven to 375°F.

Bake the pie until the top is golden brown, 25 to 30 minutes.

Allow it to cool for 10 minutes before running your knife through the presliced squares. Serve warm.

Store any leftovers in an airtight container in the refrigerator for up to 3 days, or freeze for up to 3 months. Reheat in a 350°F oven or air fryer until warmed through, about 5 minutes.

Tip for Real Life

You can either buy one twin pack of 9 × 14-inch phyllo sheets and use one pack for the bottom of the pie and one pack for the top, or buy a box of 14 × 18-inch phyllo sheets, slice the sheets down the center, and use one half for the bottom and the other for the top.

Homemade Pita Chips

We are *all* about store-bought shortcuts, but we draw the line when it comes to pita chips. You're just never going to get the same great flavor from something that comes out of the bag, not to mention the fact that you can barely even get an entire chip because they've usually all been smashed to pieces. Our solution has been, and will always be, to make our own, which takes minimal effort and yet delivers the tastiest results, especially when you're tossing your pita in a za'atar olive oil mixture before baking them to a golden crisp. Make a bunch, keep them on hand (you can even freeze them!), and dip, baby, dip.

SERVES 4 TO 6

4 (6- to 8-inch) pitas

¼ cup extra-virgin olive oil

1 teaspoon dried oregano

1 teaspoon garlic powder

½ teaspoon sweet paprika or smoked paprika

½ teaspoon fine sea salt

¼ teaspoon freshly ground black pepper

Position two oven racks in the center of the oven and preheat to 400°F.

Slice each pita into wedges. (No need to "open" the pitas first; we like to keep them doubled up so the chips are on the thicker side.) The size is up to you—smaller pieces will get crispier while larger pieces will be slightly chewier. But do make sure they are uniform so they bake evenly.

In a large bowl, stir together the olive oil, oregano, garlic powder, paprika, salt, and pepper. Add the pita wedges and give them a gentle toss until they are evenly coated in the olive oil mixture.

Spread the pita wedges in a single layer over two sheet pans, making sure there is space between them so they crisp up in the oven.

Bake until the pita chips are golden and crispy, 10 to 12 minutes, giving them a toss about halfway through. You can also rotate the pans, switching them between the racks. Keep a close eye on them—they have a habit of going quickly from perfectly crisp to overdone.

Remove from the oven and allow the pita chips to cool completely on the pan before serving or storing. They'll continue to crisp up as they cool.

Store in an airtight container at room temperature for up to 7 days. If using a resealable bag, be sure to press out all the air, which will keep moisture from getting in and making the chips chewy or stale. You can also freeze the chips in a freezer-safe container for up to 3 months. When ready to enjoy, thaw them at room temperature or reheat them in the oven for just a few minutes to restore their crispiness.

Tip for Real Life

For spicier chips, add ¼ teaspoon cayenne pepper to the olive oil mixture.

Double-Duty Dips

The brilliant thing about this chapter (if we do say so ourselves) is that all of these luscious, creamy, zippy, tangy, rich, smoky dips and dip accompaniments not only serve as a meal on their own (because, yes, dips can be dinner, too, especially when served with fresh pita and raw or cooked veggies), but they do double- or even triple-duty as meal-elevating sauces, salad dressings, and marinades. With two or three of these dips ready to go in the refrigerator, you only need to whip up a nice piece of chicken or fish or some roasted or grilled veggies or a salad or a bowl of grains to have a very satisfying dish. After all, we learned from our mama that everything's better with a dollop of baba ghanoush, hummus, tahina, or salatit zabadi—or all of them—which is what happens on our table most nights of the week.

Spicy Zhoug Sauce

Allow us to forever level up your condiment game. Meet zhoug (pronounced ts-hook), a bright, refreshing, spicy, gorgeously green sauce packed with fresh cilantro and parsley. It originated in Yemen, but it's popular throughout the entire Middle East and is what we like to think of as "Middle Eastern chimichurri." A solid multipurpose drizzle, it's excellent on roasted or grilled meat, with raw or cooked veggies, alongside hummus and pita, or drizzled over Whipped Feta (page 103). We *love* using it as a marinade for chicken and fish.

MAKES 1½ CUPS

1 bunch fresh flat-leaf parsley, leaves picked (about 1 cup packed; some stems are okay)

1 bunch fresh cilantro, leaves picked (about 1 cup packed; some stems are okay)

4 medium jalapeño peppers, stemmed and seeded (or leave the seeds if you like it spicier)

¾ cup extra-virgin olive oil

4 garlic cloves, peeled but whole

2 tablespoons fresh lime juice

1 tablespoon Aleppo pepper or red pepper flakes

1 teaspoon fine sea salt

½ teaspoon smoked paprika

½ teaspoon ground cumin

In a food processor, combine the parsley, cilantro, jalapeños, oil, garlic, lime juice, Aleppo, salt, smoked paprika, and cumin. Pulse until smooth, which is how we like ours, or leave it chunkier, if you prefer.

Store in an airtight container in the refrigerator for up to 3 days.

Make It a Meal

Some of our favorite dishes in this book for dressing up with a combination of dips and sauces are:

Mama's Beef Kofta (page 205)

Chicken Shawarma Two Ways (page 198)

Chicken Kofta Burgers (page 201)

Turkey Burger Sliders with Salatit Zabadi (page 64)

Sumac-Spiced Whole Chicken and Onions with Pitas (page 191)

Pomegranate Molasses Carrots with Chickpeas and Couscous (page 169)

Mama's Egyptian Falafel (page 40)

Middle Eastern Cottage Cheese Salad (page 42)

Egyptian Fried Steak (page 206)

And of course:

Homemade Pita Chips (page 85)

Labneh

Labneh is a cool, creamy fermented dairy spread that we grew up eating instead of yogurt. But even though it does give tangy yogurt vibes and might make you think you could get away with simply buying your favorite Greek yogurt and calling it a day, labneh is *so much better.* It's luscious, rich, and silky-smooth, adding the perfect amount of zip to sweet and savory dishes. There's honestly not a recipe in this book that couldn't be made more delicious with a dollop of labneh, but we especially love it with grilled meats, chicken, and fish, or in place of mayo on sandwiches. Just a heads-up that in order to get that perfect creamy texture, you'll need to drain the yogurt overnight.

MAKES 2½ CUPS

2 (16-ounce) containers whole-milk plain yogurt (not Greek yogurt)

½ teaspoon fine sea salt

In a large bowl, stir together the yogurt and salt.

Line a fine-mesh sieve with two layers of cheesecloth and set it over a medium bowl. Pour the yogurt into the sieve and fold up the edges of the cheesecloth over the yogurt to fully cover it.

Transfer the setup to the refrigerator and allow the yogurt to drain for 24 to 48 hours. The longer it drains, the thicker the labneh will be.

Transfer the labneh from the cheesecloth to an airtight container (discard the liquid in the bowl).

Store in the refrigerator for up to 6 days.

Roasted-Tomato Baba G

Baba ghanoush is a smoky eggplant dip, but our mom's version of baba g is anything but traditional because she adds roasted tomatoes to the mix. That hint of caramelized sweetness brings even more dimension to this rich, creamy spread that also just so happens to be dairy-free. Serve it alongside your meal or on its own with a drizzle of olive oil and some warm pitas.

MAKES 1½ CUPS

2 medium eggplants

6 tablespoons extra-virgin olive oil, plus more for serving

Fine sea salt and freshly ground black pepper

1 cup grape tomatoes

4 garlic cloves, peeled but whole

¼ cup well-stirred tahini

2 tablespoons fresh lime juice

½ teaspoon distilled white vinegar

½ teaspoon ground cumin

Finely chopped fresh flat-leaf parsley leaves, for serving

Preheat the oven to 400°F. Line a sheet pan with foil or parchment paper.

Trim the ends off the eggplants and halve the eggplants lengthwise. Use the tip of your knife to cut diagonal lines about 1 inch apart into the flesh without cutting through the skin (though it's okay if you accidentally do). Repeat on the opposite diagonal, creating a crosshatch pattern.

Place the eggplant halves on the prepared sheet pan and drizzle each with 1 tablespoon of the oil. Sprinkle with a pinch of salt and pepper and then flip them cut-side down. Bake for 15 minutes.

Carefully remove the pan from the oven and scooch the eggplant over to one side. Add the tomatoes and garlic to the clear side of the sheet pan. Drizzle them with the remaining 2 tablespoons of oil, give everything a sprinkle of salt and pepper, and spread into a single layer.

Roast until the tomatoes begin to blister and the eggplant are very soft and deflated, 25 to 30 minutes. Set aside to cool slightly.

Scoop the flesh from the eggplants into a food processor. Add the tomatoes, garlic, tahini, lime juice, vinegar, cumin, ½ teaspoon salt, and ¼ teaspoon pepper. Pulse the mixture until it has reached your desired consistency (we like it mostly smooth with just a little bit of texture).

Transfer the dip to a serving bowl, drizzle with olive oil, and sprinkle with parsley. Serve warm or at room temperature.

Store leftovers in an airtight container in the refrigerator for up to 3 days. Let the dip come to room temperature before enjoying for easier spreading and dipping.

Tip for Real Life

The texture of your baba is completely up to you. Some people like it velvety smooth, while others prefer a chunkier texture.

Silky-Smooth Hummus

We have always been on a mission to create the definitive Food Dolls signature hummus, and this one is *it*. It's silky-smooth and perfectly marries the richness of tahini with a bright pop of lime juice and smoky cumin. We've experimented a lot over the years trying to nail the perfect consistency, and we've discovered that it comes down to three things. First, cook the chickpeas with baking soda to help remove their skins, and second, start with dried chickpeas. BUT, before you go thinking that this just got a lot more complicated, we highly recommend cooking your chickpeas in a slow cooker or pressure cooker to take advantage of that hands-off time. (We've also given you a canned chickpea alternative because nothing should stand between you and a delicious bowl of hummus!) The third secret is tossing a few ice cubes in while everything blends together, which makes the texture fluffy and light.

This hummus is perfect for dipping (obviously), but also for using in sandwiches or wraps, layered under cooked veggies and proteins, dolloping on a grain bowl, or using it in place of mayo in a creamy chicken salad.

MAKES 1½ CUPS

1 pound dried chickpeas, or 2 (15-ounce) cans chickpeas, drained and thoroughly rinsed

½ teaspoon baking soda (only if using dried chickpeas)

1¼ teaspoons fine sea salt, or more as needed

⅓ cup well-stirred tahini

¼ cup fresh lime juice

3 ice cubes

2 garlic cloves, peeled but whole

1 teaspoon ground cumin

½ teaspoon freshly ground black pepper

Extra-virgin olive oil, for serving

Sumac, for serving

IF USING DRIED CHICKPEAS

Rinse them under cool water to remove any dirt or debris. Drain well and transfer the chickpeas to a slow cooker or pressure cooker; add the baking soda, ½ teaspoon of the fine sea salt, and 6 cups water.

FOR THE SLOW COOKER: Cover and cook on high for 4 hours.

FOR THE PRESSURE COOKER: Seal and pressure cook on high for 50 minutes; let the pressure naturally release for 10 to 15 minutes, then release any remaining pressure manually.

Measure out 2 cups of the chickpeas for the hummus. Store the remainder in the refrigerator or freezer.

FOR COOKED OR CANNED CHICKPEAS

Place the chickpeas in a large bowl. While rinsing under cold running water, gently rub the chickpeas to remove as many of the skins as possible. This is the key to getting the creamiest texture possible.

Transfer the chickpeas to a food processor and add the tahini, lime juice, ice cubes, garlic, cumin, pepper, and remaining ¾ teaspoon salt. Run the food processor and gradually add 1 tablespoon water. Don't be tempted to add it with the other ingredients! Slowly streaming it in helps it emulsify the hummus with the tahini and gives you that perfect texture.

Transfer the hummus to a serving bowl, drizzle with olive oil, and sprinkle with sumac.

Store in an airtight container in the refrigerator for up to 1 week.

Red Pepper Walnut Dip *(Muhammara)*

Muhammara gets its complex flavor from roasted peppers and walnuts plus a touch of tangy sweetness from pomegranate molasses. It's delicious on fresh pita and pita chips, spread over toasted ciabatta, stirred into bowls, scooped over any savory dish for any meal (try it on eggs!), and our personal favorite, tossed with pasta.

MAKES 1½ CUPS

3 medium red bell peppers

2 tablespoons extra-virgin olive oil, plus more for serving

1 cup walnuts, plus more for serving

1 slice white sandwich bread, crust removed

2 tablespoons roughly chopped fresh flat-leaf parsley leaves, plus more finely chopped for serving

1 tablespoon pomegranate molasses

1 tablespoon Aleppo pepper, or 1½ teaspoons red pepper flakes, or to taste

1 garlic clove, peeled but whole

1 teaspoon fine sea salt

¾ teaspoon smoked paprika

½ teaspoon freshly ground black pepper

Preheat the oven to 425°F. Line a sheet pan with foil or parchment paper.

Place the red bell peppers on the sheet pan. Drizzle them with 1 tablespoon of the oil and rub it all over the peppers.

Roast, turning the peppers occasionally, until they are tender and their skin is beginning to blister, 30 to 40 minutes.

Transfer the peppers to a large heatproof bowl and cover with plastic wrap. Allow the peppers to steam and cool for about 30 minutes. When cool enough to handle, peel and discard the skin under cold running water, or in a bowl of cold water, and remove and discard the stem and seeds.

While the peppers cool, in a medium skillet, toast the walnuts over medium-low heat, stirring constantly, until the nuts are slightly darker and fragrant, about 4 minutes.

In a food processor, pulse the walnuts until they're finely ground crumbs. Add the roasted red peppers, remaining 1 tablespoon oil, the bread, parsley, pomegranate molasses, Aleppo pepper, garlic, salt, smoked paprika, and black pepper. Process until the mixture is smooth.

Transfer the muhammara to a serving plate and finish with a drizzle of oil and a sprinkle of parsley and walnuts.

Store in an airtight container in the refrigerator for up to 6 days.

Yogurt Toum,
page 111

Silky-Smooth Hummus,
page 94

Mama's Egyptian
Falafel (Ta'ameya),
page 40

Egyptian Tomato and
Cucumber Salad
(Salata Baladi), page 145

Salatit Zabadi
(Cucumber Yogurt
Salad), page 101

Sumac Onions,
page 102

Egyptian Fava Bean Salad
(Ful Medames with Tahini),
page 58

Red Pepper
Walnut Dip
(Muhammara),
page 95

Herby Roasted
Olives,
page 104

Middle Eastern
Pickled Cucumber
(Khiyar Mikhalil)
page 115

Middle Eastern Pico *(Dakous)*

Our late great-aunt Tahiya, who lived in Saudi Arabia, would always make this fresh salsa to serve with rice and grilled meats whenever she'd come to Egypt for a visit. We've since come to think of dakous as a sort of Middle Eastern pico de gallo, namely because the super-fresh flavors are so similar, from tomatoes, jalapeño, herbs, and lime juice. That said, the texture of this preparation is closer to a sauce, making it ideal for pouring over all the things. In addition to giving any dish just the right amount of heat and acid, we also love using dakous as a marinade for chicken and fish. And there's usually a bowlful ready to go with Homemade Pita Chips (page 85) whenever we have company. Because the flavors continue to meld as the salsa sits, we highly recommend making a batch on a Sunday so you can use it all week.

MAKES 1½ CUPS

3 medium Roma tomatoes, quartered

1 medium jalapeño pepper, stemmed and seeded (or leave the seeds in for more heat)

¼ cup fresh flat-leaf parsley leaves

¼ cup fresh cilantro leaves

1 small shallot, roughly chopped

2 tablespoons fresh lime juice

2 garlic cloves, minced

½ teaspoon fine sea salt

¼ teaspoon freshly ground black pepper

In a food processor, combine the tomatoes, jalapeño, parsley, cilantro, shallot, lime juice, garlic, salt, and pepper. Pulse until the mixture is finely chopped. You still want to see distinct pieces of each ingredient.

Store the salsa in an airtight container in the refrigerator for up to 1 week.

Baba's Tahina Sauce

Our dad, or baba, is always eager to lend a hand in the kitchen—especially in the role of "Master Taste Tester," a title he has given himself and takes very seriously. (Sometimes a little too seriously; the honesty can be brutal!) When we had him try our version of the beloved and sacred tahini sauce—or tahina (the Arabic pronunciation)—he sampled and tweaked until we nailed just the right amount of acidity, spice, and smoky cumin. (Turns out his secret is a little bit of Greek yogurt, which isn't traditional but adds a welcome brightness and lightness.) It was worth the effort because tahina is a true multipurpose staple that we will always have in the refrigerator and is often on our table no matter the meal. It's almost like hummus's lesser-known cousin because of how similar in flavor they are, but we have to admit that tahina sauce has the edge in our book when it comes to being able to quickly throw together a batch for drizzling over everything, from your morning falafel or ful to your chicken shawarma and kofta, to your salads, soups, and bowls. There's not a lot that tahina can't do.

MAKES ¾ CUP

¼ cup plus 2 tablespoons well-stirred tahini

¼ cup whole-milk plain Greek yogurt

2 tablespoons fresh lime juice

1 tablespoon distilled white vinegar

1 medium garlic clove, grated

1½ teaspoons ground cumin

½ teaspoon fine sea salt

Cayenne pepper

In a large bowl, combine the tahini, yogurt, lime juice, vinegar, garlic, cumin, salt, and a pinch of cayenne. Add ½ cup water and whisk until the mixture is completely smooth. (Alternatively, you could do this in a blender or food processor.) Taste and adjust the heat level by adding more cayenne, if desired.

Store in an airtight container in the refrigerator for up to 1 week.

Tip for Real Life

Tahina traditionally has a light, runny texture like salad dressing. But if you prefer a thicker dip-like consistency, simply decrease the amount of water. Remember, you can always start with less and gradually add more as desired.

Salatit Zabadi *(Cucumber Yogurt Salad)*

Okay, we know we've said this about pretty much every other recipe in this chapter—and we're not exaggerating—but this is truly a must-have condiment for the table. If you're familiar with Greek tzatziki, which has the same tang-ifying, cream-ifying effect on everything it's dolloped on and swirled into, then you already have an idea of how amazing this Egyptian rendition is. The biggest difference is that our version has bits of cucumber (versus grated), which gives it great texture, plus just a bit of sour cream for that extra brightness. It somehow manages to make everything it's served with taste ten times better.

MAKES 1½ CUPS

1 medium Persian or ¼ English cucumber

1 cup whole-milk plain yogurt

2 tablespoons sour cream

1 teaspoon dried mint

½ teaspoon fine sea salt

¼ teaspoon freshly ground black pepper

Fresh mint leaves, for serving

Peel the cucumber and halve it lengthwise. If using an English cucumber, use a spoon to gently scoop out the seeds and discard them (or eat them!), then chop the cucumber into ¼-inch pieces. Measure out ½ cup of the chopped cucumber for this recipe (enjoy the rest as a cook's treat).

In a medium bowl, stir together the yogurt, sour cream, mint, salt, and pepper. Add the cucumbers and gently fold them into the mixture until just combined. Cover the sauce and refrigerate for at least 30 minutes before serving. Sprinkle with mint and serve.

Store in an airtight container in the refrigerator for up to 3 days.

Tip for Real Life

When using dried mint, rub it between your fingers or palms first to help release the oils.

Sumac Onions

These spice- and vinegar-marinated onions fall somewhere between a pickle and a slaw—they're our go-to secret sauce. You'd never expect that a pile of raw onions could be so deliciously savory and complexly flavorful on their own, but you'll rarely find kebabs, shawarma, wraps, or sandwiches without them on our tables. We highly recommend keeping a jar in the fridge and adding a tuft of them—plus a sprinkle of their brine—onto savory dishes and spreads.

MAKES 4 CUPS

2 medium red onions, halved and thinly sliced

½ cup finely chopped fresh flat-leaf parsley

1 tablespoon distilled white vinegar, plus more to taste

1 tablespoon extra-virgin olive oil

1 tablespoon ground sumac

1 teaspoon fine sea salt

¼ teaspoon freshly ground black pepper

Add the onions to a large bowl. Use your hands or a fork to gently separate the layers of onions. Add the parsley, vinegar, olive oil, sumac, salt, and pepper and toss well to combine. If you like things on the tangier side, taste and add a splash more vinegar, if needed.

Cover the bowl with plastic wrap and refrigerate for at least 30 minutes before serving as a condiment or topping.

Store in an airtight container in the refrigerator for up to 3 days.

Tips for Real Life

We like red onions for this preparation because of their mild, sweet flavor and vibrant color, but you could use white or yellow onions instead.

There are as many variations of this preparation as there are Egyptians, so there's no rule about how much sumac, parsley, or vinegar go into the mix. Every time you make a batch, feel free to change up the ratios.

Whipped Feta

Feta is a sheep's and/or goat's milk cheese that is creamy, briny perfection in its own right. But when whipped in a food processor or blender with a little sour cream, garlic, and lemon juice, it reaches a whole new level of tangy-rich deliciousness. It's one of our favorite multipurpose spreads because it can be a quick appetizer with pita (chips or bread), crackers, or raw veggies; or it can be heaped with cooked vegetables, meat, or fish for an effortless meal with layer-upon-layer of punchy flavor. We also love topping it with roasted things, like olives, cauliflower, or tomatoes, or cooked chickpeas for a more-pulled-together (but still extremely easy) starter, snack, or side.

MAKES ABOUT 2½ CUPS
(SERVES 8 AS A STARTER)

8 ounces brine-packed feta cheese

8 ounces cream cheese, at room temperature

⅓ cup sour cream

2 tablespoons milk of your choice or water

Juice of ½ lemon (about 2 tablespoons)

1 tablespoon extra-virgin olive oil, plus more for serving

2 medium garlic cloves, peeled but whole

½ teaspoon fine sea salt, plus more to taste

½ teaspoon freshly ground black pepper, plus more to taste

In a food processor or blender, combine the feta, cream cheese, sour cream, milk, lemon juice, olive oil, garlic, salt, and pepper. Process until completely smooth. If using a blender, you may need to pause occasionally to scrape down the sides with a spatula. Season with more salt and pepper to taste, if desired.

Spoon the creamy feta into a serving bowl or spread it over a platter and add your desired toppings. Drizzle with a little more olive oil and serve.

Store in an airtight container in the refrigerator for up to 4 days.

Tips for Real Life

If you prefer an even stronger garlicky flavor, add up to 5 garlic cloves.

For a salty-sweet spread, add 1 tablespoon honey with the rest of the ingredients.

Try adding cubed watermelon and fresh mint over the top for a refreshing salad; drizzling it over roasted vegetables for a vegetarian side or main; serving alongside Sumac Chicken Wings (page 67) or Mama's Beef Kofta (page 205); or spreading it on top of naan or pita in place of the whipped ricotta for the Med Pizzas (page 161).

Meal Makers & Spotlight Takers

Each of these "toppers" transforms whatever it's spooned over into something really special and, of course, tasty. They would be great spooned over Whipped Feta (page 103), hummus, or any of the proteins, grains, or veg dishes in this book.

Herby Roasted Olives

Olives get deeply savory when roasted, which is why we love tossing them with shallots and herbs to make an extremely satisfying yet extremely simple topping for Silky-Smooth Hummus (page 94) or Labneh (page 91). But you could also add these to your favorite salad, pasta, veg, meat, or fish dish to level up the flavor and sophistication factors. Or serve them on their own as a snack.

MAKES 2 CUPS (SERVES 8)

6 ounces (¾ cup) pitted green olives, such as Manzanilla

6 ounces (¾ cup) pitted Kalamata olives

3 medium shallots, sliced lengthwise

2 tablespoons extra-virgin olive oil

2 teaspoons dried thyme

2 teaspoons dried oregano

½ teaspoon fine sea salt

½ teaspoon freshly ground black pepper

Preheat the oven to 400°F.

In a medium baking dish, combine the green olives, Kalamata olives, shallots, olive oil, thyme, oregano, salt, and pepper and toss to coat.

Bake, without stirring, until the olives and shallots are completely tender, 25 to 30 minutes.

Set aside to cool slightly before serving. Store in an airtight container in the refrigerator for up to 3 days.

Smoky Roasted Cauliflower

Is it a vegetable side? An appetizer? Lunch? There's really no wrong answer here. And if you don't consider yourself a cauliflower lover, then you haven't tried our roasted version with plenty of smoked paprika.

SERVES 4

1 (16-ounce) bag cauliflower florets, or 1 medium head cauliflower, cut into 1-inch pieces (about 4 cups)

3 tablespoons extra-virgin olive oil, plus more for serving

2 teaspoons smoked paprika

½ teaspoon fine sea salt

¼ teaspoon freshly ground black pepper

Finely chopped fresh flat-leaf parsley leaves, for serving

Aleppo pepper or red pepper flakes, for serving

Za'atar, for serving

Preheat the oven to 400°F.

In a 9 × 13-inch baking dish, combine the cauliflower, olive oil, smoked paprika, salt, and black pepper. Toss until the cauliflower is evenly coated.

Roast, without stirring, until the cauliflower is tender and lightly browned, 25 to 30 minutes.

Set aside to cool before serving. Finish with a drizzle of olive oil and a sprinkle of parsley, Aleppo, and za'atar.

Marinated Chickpeas

Chickpeas are like little sponges because they take on flavor so well. Especially this herbed, spiced marinade—after just 30 minutes, they become the ultimate meal-maker, whether you're spooning them over Labneh (page 91), Greek yogurt, Silky-Smooth Hummus (page 94), or any soup or salad.

SERVES 8

3 tablespoons extra-virgin olive oil

3 tablespoons finely chopped fresh cilantro leaves

1 teaspoon dried oregano

½ teaspoon smoked paprika

½ teaspoon fine sea salt

½ teaspoon freshly ground black pepper

2 (15-ounce) cans chickpeas, drained and thoroughly rinsed, or 3 cups cooked chickpeas

In a medium bowl, whisk together the olive oil, cilantro, oregano, smoked paprika, salt, and pepper. Stir in the chickpeas and allow the mixture to marinate for at least 30 minutes. Or transfer the mixture to an airtight container and marinate in the refrigerator for up to 3 days.

Yogurt Toum

Toum is a Lebanese sauce that's essentially Middle Eastern mayo with a serious garlicky kick. Neither of us is a huge fan of the traditional version's intense raw garlic flavor, nor do we love seeing how much oil actually goes into this emulsion, so we took matters into our own hands. This recipe swaps the oil for a lighter yogurt-mayo mix and includes just enough garlic to keep it interesting but not give you dragon breath. There are very few things that wouldn't be delicious with a schmear of toum, but noteworthy uses are sandwiches, warm pita, a dollop stirred into pastas and soups, as a dip for veggies, served alongside grilled or roasted meats and veggies, and French fries (ketchup who?).

MAKES 1¼ CUPS

1 large garlic clove, peeled

1 tablespoon fresh lemon juice

1 cup whole-milk plain yogurt

3 tablespoons mayonnaise

½ teaspoon fine sea salt

¼ teaspoon ground white pepper

Grate the garlic into a small bowl. (A Microplane is great for this.) Stir in the lemon juice and allow the mixture to sit for 10 minutes. This will help mellow the heat of the garlic.

Add the yogurt, mayonnaise, salt, and white pepper to the same bowl. Mix all the ingredients together until well combined. Refrigerate until you're ready to serve.

Store in an airtight container in the fridge for up to 1 week.

Tips for Real Life

For a more intense garlic flavor, skip soaking the grated garlic in lemon juice.

For a thicker sauce, sub in Greek yogurt or Labneh (page 91) for the yogurt.

We call for using white pepper here so you don't see flecks of black pepper in the sauce, but if black pepper's all you have, you'll still have some very delicious toum!

Pickled Roasted Eggplant Salad *(Betengan Mekhalel)*

In Egypt, if we're eating fish, then we're also having betengan mekhalel, a smoky, jammy eggplant salad spiked with briny vinegar. But don't let that limit you when you want to tuck into this versatile condiment-side combo. It's equally delicious spooned over grilled meats and scooped up with pita. We love keeping a batch in the fridge because the flavors continue to develop and meld as the salad marinates itself.

SERVES 4

ROASTED EGGPLANT

Olive oil, for the pan

1 large eggplant

3 tablespoons extra-virgin olive oil

½ teaspoon sweet paprika

½ teaspoon garlic powder

½ teaspoon fine sea salt

¼ teaspoon freshly ground black pepper

BRINE

½ medium green bell pepper, roughly chopped

1 small jalapeño pepper (optional), stemmed, seeded (or leave the seeds in if you want more heat), and roughly chopped

1 medium garlic clove, peeled but whole

2 tablespoons distilled white vinegar

½ teaspoon fine sea salt

ROAST THE EGGPLANT: Preheat the oven to 425°F. Line a sheet pan with foil and evenly coat it with about a teaspoon of olive oil.

Peel the eggplant and cut it crosswise into ½-inch-thick rounds. Arrange the slices on the prepared sheet pan in a single layer.

In a small bowl, whisk together the 3 tablespoons olive oil, the paprika, garlic powder, salt, and pepper. Brush the mixture over the top of the eggplant to coat each piece.

Roast the eggplant for 15 minutes. Then carefully flip and roast for another 10 minutes, or until the eggplant is tender and slightly browned.

MEANWHILE, MAKE THE BRINE: In a food processor, combine the bell pepper, jalapeño (if using), garlic, vinegar, and salt. Pulse until the mixture is finely chopped but not pureed.

Arrange the roasted eggplant slices on a serving platter and drizzle them with the brine. Cover the dish with plastic wrap and transfer the dish to the refrigerator to chill for at least 1 hour or up to overnight. The longer it sits, the better it gets.

Store any leftovers in an airtight container in the refrigerator for up to 4 days.

Tips for Real Life

Do your best to make the eggplant slices the same thickness so they cook evenly.

Keep an eye on the eggplant as it roasts to ensure that it doesn't burn. You want the eggplant tender but not mushy.

Instead of distilled white vinegar, you could also use apple cider vinegar, which adds a slightly fruity tang.

Tips for Real Life

Make sure your cucumbers are firm to the touch, which will guarantee nice, crisp pickles.

White vinegar lends a sharp, classically pickle-y flavor while apple cider vinegar has mellower, fruitier acidity. Experiment to see which you like better, or even use a combination of the two!

For extra-crunchy pickles, add a canned grape leaf to the jar. They contain tannins, which help maintain the fresh snap of the cucumbers. You can find them at Middle Eastern grocery stores or online.

Feel free to play around with the spices and herbs. You can add mustard seeds, dill seeds, or cloves. Use extra chiles, or use Aleppo pepper or red pepper flakes instead of fresh chile. Or use dried herbs instead of fresh (just use one-third of the original amount of fresh called for). So long as you preserve the ratios of vinegar to water and salt to sugar—which will ensure proper preservation and flavor—you're free to take liberties.

You could also use a different sweetener, such as honey or agave syrup.

Middle Eastern Pickled Cucumbers *(Khiyar Mikhalil)*

Whenever you order a Middle Eastern mezze platter, aka dip and condiment heaven served with a stack of warm, fluffy pita, you'll also almost always get a little dish of garlicky, spiced pickles. These pickles were a part of our regular dinner spreads, too, namely because traditional Egyptian meals usually include at least one pickled item to bring that extra boost of brightness and acidity to any savory dish. Now we love serving them alongside dips and spreads, but also enjoying them as you would a classic dill pickle—with sandwiches and burgers, or even diced and folded into tuna and chicken salad.

MAKES ABOUT 2 CUPS

5 medium pickling or Persian cucumbers, ends trimmed and cut into ½-inch-thick spears or rounds

1 fresh red chile, such as Fresno or cayenne, stemmed and sliced (seeded for less heat, or omit entirely)

2 tablespoons roughly chopped fresh mint leaves

2 tablespoons roughly chopped fresh dill

1 cup distilled white vinegar or apple cider vinegar

2 tablespoons fine sea salt

2 tablespoons sugar

6 medium garlic cloves, lightly crushed and peeled

1 tablespoon coriander seeds

1 teaspoon cumin seeds

1 teaspoon black peppercorns

Bring a large pot of water to a boil. Add a 1-quart heatproof canning jar and its lid and boil for 10 minutes to sterilize. Use tongs to carefully remove the jar and lid and allow them to air-dry on a wire rack or kitchen towel.

Tightly pack the cucumber into the cooled jar, interspersing them with the chile (if using), mint, and dill. Set aside.

In a medium pot, combine 2 cups water, the vinegar, salt, sugar, garlic, coriander, cumin, and peppercorns. Bring to a simmer over medium heat, stirring occasionally, and simmer until the salt and sugar are fully dissolved, about 2 minutes.

Carefully pour the brine over the cucumbers, ensuring they are completely submerged. (Otherwise, the exposed bits will go rancid.) You can use a piece of onion or other vegetable to weight them down if you're having trouble with them bobbing to the surface. The brine should not come up further than the top ½ inch of the jar. If it does, pour off some of the brine.

Allow the jar to cool to room temperature, uncovered, then tightly seal with the lid. Refrigerate the pickles for at least 48 hours to let the cucumbers soak up all the flavor and do their pickling thing. The longer they sit, the more flavor they'll develop. Be sure to use a clean utensil when spearing the pickles from the jar to avoid contamination.

Store in the fridge for up to 2 months.

Pretty Delicious Salads

We always like to say that we follow the 80/20 rule, meaning that most of our meals are going to be based around whole, nutrient-packed foods—but with enough room for the occasional bowl of sticky toffee pudding or cookies 'n' cream pots de crème. And because we spend most of our days testing recipes (aka attempting not to eat the entire pan of creamy chicken spaghetti bake), we need easy stand-by dishes that can be ready in a moment's notice, fill us up, and yet leave us feeling a little lighter and brighter. And those dishes, more often than not, are salads. But we're not talking about a sad little bowl of wimpy lettuce and dressing. No, these dishes are the main event, layered with bold punches of texture, color, and flavor and loaded up with your favorite ingredients, making each of these salads a one-and-done meal. If you make the dressings ahead of time, you can throw any of these salads together whenever the mood or the need strikes.

Quinoa Tabbouleh with Lime Vinaigrette

You won't find many Mediterranean spreads without tabbouleh, a grain salad loaded with crisp veggies and herbs and bathed in a bright vinaigrette. We've tweaked things slightly by swapping out the traditional bulgur wheat for quinoa—one of our favorite nongrain grains (it's technically a seed)—and amping up the sunshine factor by using fresh lime juice in the dressing. It's great as a main or a side, and it feels like good habits in a bowl—without tasting like it. Just keep in mind that it's best served chilled or at room temperature, so consider making the quinoa at the beginning of the week so it's ready to go.

SERVES 4

1 cup white quinoa

LIME VINAIGRETTE

¼ cup extra-virgin olive oil

Juice of 2 limes (about ¼ cup)

½ teaspoon fine sea salt, plus more to taste

½ teaspoon freshly ground black pepper, plus more to taste

QUINOA SALAD

2 cups packed finely chopped fresh flat-leaf parsley leaves

1 heaping cup diced tomatoes (about 4 medium Romas)

1 cup chopped cucumber (about 3 medium Persian or 1 seeded and peeled English cucumber)

4 green onions, both white and green parts, finely chopped (about ¾ cup)

¼ cup packed finely chopped fresh mint leaves

Cook the quinoa according to the package directions. Cool to room temperature before proceeding.

MAKE THE LIME VINAIGRETTE: In a small bowl or screw-top jar, combine the olive oil, lime juice, salt, and pepper. Whisk or shake until the dressing is completely smooth and emulsified. Season with more salt and/or pepper, if desired.

ASSEMBLE THE QUINOA SALAD: In a large bowl, combine the parsley, tomatoes, cooled quinoa, cucumbers, green onions, and mint. Gently toss to combine. Drizzle on the dressing to taste and once again toss until well incorporated. Cover the bowl with plastic wrap and refrigerate for at least 30 minutes or up to 2 hours to chill the salad and allow the flavors to meld.

When ready to serve, give the salad one more toss.

MAKE IT AHEAD

You can cook the quinoa and prepare the dressing up to 5 days in advance and store them in sealed containers in the refrigerator. When you're ready to assemble the salad, chop the veggies and herbs and toss everything together.

Tip for Real Life

Feel free to swap out the quinoa for ½ cup fine bulgur—which doesn't even need to be cooked! Instead of dicing the tomatoes, finely chop them and sprinkle with salt and pepper. Add the drained and thoroughly rinsed bulgur, mix well, and set aside for 15 minutes. The bulgur will soften and plump as it sits in the tomato juices.

Watermelon Salad with Feta Crema

Summer days at the lake bring one thing to mind for us: watermelon. And the only thing better than the juicy-sweet hunks our mom would put out for everyone on hot afternoons was the big cubes of creamy, salty feta and doughy pita that she'd serve alongside them. Ours has the same laid-back vibe as the original, just dressed up a touch with ribbons of feta crema, sumac-dusted pita chips, and a hint of fresh mint. It's as refreshing as it is satisfying, and there's not a barbecue, potluck, or picnic that would be complete without it.

SERVES 4

1 (4-ounce) block brine-packed feta cheese

3 tablespoons sour cream

1 tablespoon heavy cream

½ teaspoon ground sumac

4 cups cubed seedless watermelon (1-inch pieces; about ½ medium watermelon)

¾ cup roughly chopped sumac-dusted pita chips (from Fattoush, page 143) or store-bought pita chips

6 fresh mint leaves, roughly chopped

2 teaspoons Aleppo pepper or red pepper flakes

MAKE IT AHEAD

The feta crema can be made ahead and stored in an airtight container in the refrigerator for up to 3 days.

In a blender or food processor, combine the feta, sour cream, heavy cream, and sumac. Process until the mixture is smooth and creamy. If necessary, add up to 1 tablespoon water until the mixture is nice and drizzly.

Arrange the watermelon on a serving platter. Add the pita chips on top, then drizzle the feta crema over everything, followed by a sprinkling of the mint and Aleppo. Serve immediately.

Southwest Salad with Fajita-Style Peppers & Creamy Jalapeño-Lime Dressing

One of the things we love most about a good, hearty salad is that it's everything you need—and want—in one bowl. This recipe is the perfect example of how there's nothing wimpy or skimpy about dishes in this category, especially when you're not limiting your salad to lettuce. Here we're taking smoky charred peppers and layering them over cilantro-scented rice and beans, then smothering everything with a creamy, tangy dressing packing a kick of green heat.

SERVES 6

FAJITA-STYLE PEPPERS

1 medium red bell pepper, thinly sliced

1 medium green bell pepper, thinly sliced

1 small red onion, thinly sliced

2 tablespoons extra-virgin olive oil

1 teaspoon chile powder

1 teaspoon dried oregano

1 teaspoon fine sea salt

½ teaspoon smoked paprika

½ teaspoon freshly ground black pepper

CREAMY JALAPEÑO-LIME DRESSING

½ cup sour cream

½ cup packed fresh cilantro leaves

¼ cup extra-virgin olive oil

1 medium jalapeño pepper, stemmed and seeded (or leave the seeds in if you want more heat)

1 green onion, both white and green parts, roughly chopped

Juice of 1 lime (about 2 tablespoons)

1 medium garlic clove, peeled but whole

1 tablespoon honey

1 teaspoon ground cumin

1 teaspoon fine sea salt, plus more to taste

SALAD

Cilantro-Lime Rice (page 229)

6 cups greens of your choice (we like mixed greens, arugula, or romaine)

1 (15-ounce) can black beans, drained and thoroughly rinsed

2 cups corn kernels (we use thawed frozen corn)

1 medium avocado, diced

MAKE IT AHEAD

The dressing can be made ahead and stored in an airtight container in the refrigerator for up to 1 week.

MAKE THE FAJITA-STYLE PEPPERS: Preheat the oven to 400°F. Line a sheet pan with foil or parchment paper.

Arrange the bell peppers and onion on the sheet pan. In a small bowl, stir together the olive oil, chile powder, oregano, salt, smoked paprika, and black pepper. Drizzle the mixture over the peppers and onion and use your hands to ensure everything is well coated. Spread the veggies in an even layer over the sheet pan.

Roast until the vegetables are tender and beginning to caramelize in places, about 20 minutes, tossing about halfway through. Remove from the oven and set aside.

MEANWHILE, MAKE THE CREAMY JALAPEÑO-LIME DRESSING: In a food processor or blender, combine the sour cream, cilantro, olive oil, jalapeño, green onion, lime juice, garlic, honey, cumin, and salt. Process until the mixture is smooth, adding up to 1 tablespoon water, if needed, so the dressing is thick but drizzly. Adjust the seasoning with more salt, if desired.

ASSEMBLE THE SALAD: Spread the rice over the bottom of a serving platter or large bowl. Top with the greens, black beans, corn, fajita peppers, and avocado. Drizzle as much dressing over the salad as you like and give everything a gentle toss to combine.

Tips for Real Life

You could skip the greens and make this more of a fajita bowl.

This is a hearty main dish, but you could also add a protein, such as chicken or shrimp. We love making a batch of the shrimp from our Mediterranean Cobb Salad (page 141).

Feel free to substitute plain white or brown rice for the cilantro-lime rice.

Marinated Roasted Veggie Orzo

When you roast zucchini, bell peppers, and eggplant until they're falling-apart tender and then let them soak up a lemon-herb vinaigrette, these veg go from supporting cast to main characters. Tossing pasta—in this case rice-shaped orzo—into the mix puts this squarely in whole-meal territory. Think meal prep, potlucks, barbecues, and any other spread where you need a durable room-temp dish.

SERVES 6 TO 8

ROASTED VEGETABLES

2 medium zucchinis, cut into 1-inch pieces

1 globe eggplant (about 8 ounces), cut into 1-inch cubes

1 medium red bell pepper, cut into 1-inch pieces

1 medium green bell pepper, cut into 1-inch pieces

1 medium red onion, sliced

¼ cup extra-virgin olive oil

3 medium garlic cloves, minced

1 teaspoon fine sea salt

1 teaspoon freshly ground black pepper

LEMON-HERB DRESSING

⅓ cup extra-virgin olive oil

¼ cup fresh lemon juice

3 medium garlic cloves, minced

1 teaspoon dried oregano

1 teaspoon dried thyme

1 teaspoon Aleppo pepper or red pepper flakes

½ teaspoon fine sea salt

½ teaspoon freshly ground black pepper

PASTA SALAD

1 pound orzo

⅓ cup packed roughly chopped fresh basil leaves

1 (4-ounce) block brine-packed feta cheese (optional), crumbled, for serving

ROAST THE VEGETABLES: Preheat the oven to 450°F. Line a sheet pan with foil or parchment paper.

Place the zucchini, eggplant, bell peppers, and onion on the prepared sheet pan. Drizzle with the olive oil and sprinkle with the garlic, salt, and black pepper. Give everything a good toss to ensure all the vegetables are well coated. Spread the vegetables into an even layer. (You may need a second sheet pan; you don't want the veggies too crowded or they'll end up steaming instead of caramelizing.)

Roast until tender and beginning to char in places, about 25 minutes, tossing halfway through.

MEANWHILE, MAKE THE LEMON-HERB DRESSING: In a medium bowl or screw-top jar, combine the olive oil, lemon juice, garlic, oregano, thyme, Aleppo, salt, and black pepper. Whisk or shake well until the dressing is smooth and emulsified. Set aside.

Transfer the vegetables (including any juices from the sheet pan) to a large bowl. Pour in half of the dressing, toss to combine, and allow the vegetables to marinate for 30 minutes.

ASSEMBLE THE SALAD: While the vegetables marinate, cook the pasta according to package directions. Drain and let cool slightly before returning the pasta to the pot.

Add the marinated vegetables (including any juices from the bowl) to the pasta along with the basil and fold to evenly incorporate. Transfer the salad to a serving bowl and drizzle with more dressing to taste. If desired, sprinkle with the feta. Let the pasta sit for at least 15 minutes before serving for the orzo to cool to room temperature and the flavors to meld. If you have the time, let the pasta sit for at least 1 hour, which is what we prefer if we can.

Store in an airtight container in the refrigerator for up to 5 days. Allow the salad to come to room temperature before serving.

Quinoa & Butternut Squash Salad with Honey-Dijon Vinaigrette

As soon as the first fall leaves hit the ground, our sweaters come out of the storage, the pumpkin spice latte order goes in, and this salad enters the conversation. It's a classic grain salad with roasted squash, but what really puts it over the edge flavor-wise is slathering the squash in herbed pomegranate molasses before it roasts. This tangy, syrupy magic twist brings out the squash's natural sugars, giving it even deeper custardy flavor. With chopped apples, pomegranate seeds, dried cherries, and feta cheese sprinkled over the top, it's a salad as cozy as it is refined—perfect for the Thanksgiving table or lunch on a Wednesday.

SERVES 6 TO 8

1 cup quinoa

ROASTED SQUASH

6 cups cubed butternut squash (from 1 large squash)

3 tablespoons extra-virgin olive oil

2 tablespoons pomegranate molasses

½ teaspoon dried thyme

½ teaspoon fine sea salt

½ teaspoon freshly ground black pepper

HONEY-DIJON VINAIGRETTE

½ cup extra-virgin olive oil

3 tablespoons apple cider vinegar

2 tablespoons fresh lemon juice (from ½ lemon)

2 tablespoons honey

2 teaspoons Dijon mustard

1 medium garlic clove, grated

1 teaspoon Aleppo pepper or red pepper flakes

½ teaspoon fine sea salt

SALAD

6 cups packed mixed lettuces and greens (we love a mix of green leaf, red leaf, arugula, and sometimes chard)

1 large apple, such as Honeycrisp, Fuji, or Gala, cored and chopped (we leave the peel on)

½ cup crumbled brine-packed feta cheese

½ cup pomegranate seeds

½ cup chopped walnuts or pecans, or sliced or slivered almonds, toasted (see Dry-Toasting, page 29)

¼ cup dried cherries

Tip for Real Life

You can swap out the quinoa for any other grain you like, such as farro or brown rice, cooked according to the package directions.

Cook the quinoa according to the package directions. Set aside for at least 15 minutes to cool slightly.

Preheat the oven to 400°F. Line a sheet pan with foil or parchment paper.

ROAST THE SQUASH: Place the squash on the prepared sheet pan. In a small bowl, stir together the olive oil, pomegranate molasses, thyme, salt, and black pepper. Drizzle the mixture over the squash and give it a good toss to ensure all of the squash is well coated. Spread the squash into an even layer.

Roast until the squash is tender and slightly caramelized, 20 to 25 minutes, stirring midway through. Set aside to cool slightly.

MEANWHILE, MAKE THE DRESSING: In a medium bowl or screw-top jar, combine the olive oil, vinegar, lemon juice, honey, mustard, garlic, Aleppo, and salt. Whisk or shake vigorously until the dressing is creamy and emulsified. Set aside.

ASSEMBLE THE SALAD: In a large bowl, combine the roasted squash, quinoa, greens, apple, feta, pomegranate seeds, toasted walnuts, and cherries.

Drizzle over as much dressing as you prefer (we use about three-quarters of it and serve the remaining on the side for those who want more) and toss to combine.

Pear, Fig & Arugula Salad with Farro

Farro is a chewy, earthy, nutty grain that holds its own in the flavor and texture department but also plays nicely with others. We especially love layering it with spicy arugula, sweet pears and figs, and tangy goat cheese for a deceptively simple salad that feels really luxe. That said, if you're not serving this for a fall brunch or holiday dinner, it's perfectly acceptable to devour this on the couch in your sweats.

SERVES 6 TO 8

SALAD

1 cup farro

10 ounces baby arugula

2 medium Anjou pears, cored and thinly sliced (we leave the peel on)

1 cup sliced fresh figs (6 to 8 figs)

½ medium red onion, thinly sliced

4 ounces fresh goat cheese, crumbled

½ cup salted roasted pistachios

DIJON VINAIGRETTE

¼ cup extra-virgin olive oil

Juice of 1 lime (about 2 tablespoons)

1 tablespoon honey

2 teaspoons Dijon mustard

1½ teaspoons dried oregano

1 medium garlic clove, minced

½ teaspoon fine sea salt

½ teaspoon freshly ground black pepper

MAKE THE SALAD: Cook the farro according to the package directions. Drain and set aside for at least 15 minutes to cool.

In a large salad bowl, combine the arugula, pears, figs, onion, goat cheese, and pistachios and set aside.

MAKE THE DIJON VINAIGRETTE: In a medium bowl or screw-top jar, combine the olive oil, lime juice, honey, mustard, oregano, garlic, salt, and pepper. Whisk or shake vigorously until the dressing is creamy and emulsified.

Add the cooled farro to the bowl with the arugula and drizzle with dressing to taste. Give everything a gentle toss until well combined and coated with the dressing.

Tip for Real Life

This would also be delicious made with quinoa, barley, or brown rice as the base.

MAKE IT AHEAD

To prep the salad in advance, you can chop all the ingredients except for the pears (they should be chopped fresh) and store them individually in containers in the refrigerator for up to 3 days. The dressing can be stored in an airtight container in the refrigerator for up to 1 week. Assemble the salad when you're ready to eat.

Pasta Salad with Green Goddess Dressing

Minnesota is the unofficial pasta salad capital—it is near impossible to find a cookout, picnic, or potluck where there's not a giant bowlful, usually tossed with ample mayo and a few stray veggies. No disrespect to this classic dish, but even pasta salad wants to feel a little more elegant sometimes. So we've given her a sophisticated (but no less delicious) makeover with an herb-packed dressing, which blends mayo with mild, creamy mascarpone cheese. It's a glow-up for sure, but still with that quintessential summer-in-a-bowl feel.

SERVES 8

PASTA

Fine sea salt

1 pound rotini pasta

1 pound frozen green peas

GREEN GODDESS DRESSING

½ cup mayonnaise

½ cup packed fresh basil leaves

½ cup packed fresh flat-leaf parsley leaves

½ cup mascarpone cheese

1 medium jalapeño pepper, stemmed and seeded (or leave the seeds in if you want more heat)

Juice of ½ lemon (about 2 tablespoons)

2 medium garlic cloves, peeled but whole

1 tablespoon white wine vinegar

1½ teaspoons fine sea salt

SALAD

½ cup sliced pitted Kalamata olives

⅓ cup thinly sliced oil-packed sun-dried tomatoes, drained

4 ounces Gouda cheese, cut into ½-inch cubes

2 green onions, both white and green parts, finely chopped

Fresh basil leaves, torn, for serving

Fine sea salt and freshly ground black pepper, to taste

MAKE THE PASTA: Bring a large pot of water to a boil over medium-high heat. Add a generous pinch of salt and add the pasta. Cook to al dente according to the package directions, adding the peas during the final 1 minute of cooking. Drain and rinse the pasta and peas under cold water. Set aside to cool slightly.

MEANWHILE, MAKE THE GREEN GODDESS DRESSING: In a food processor or blender, combine the mayo, basil, parsley, mascarpone, jalapeño, lemon juice, garlic, vinegar, and salt. Process until the mixture is completely smooth.

ASSEMBLE THE SALAD: In a large serving bowl, combine the pasta and peas, olives, sun-dried tomatoes, Gouda, and green onions. Pour the dressing over the top to taste and gently toss until everything is well coated. Season with salt and pepper to taste.

Cover the bowl with plastic wrap and refrigerate the salad for at least 30 minutes or up to 3 days before serving. (We think it tastes freshest the day it's made, but we get that convenience is queen!) Serve chilled or at room temperature garnished with fresh basil.

MAKE IT AHEAD

Assemble the salad and store it in an airtight container in the refrigerator for up to 3 days.

Tip for Real Life

Bell peppers, baby spinach, baby arugula, and blanched broccoli (quickly boiled until it is bright green and barely tender and then immediately cooled in ice water) would all be tasty folded into this salad.

Tahini Caesar with Pita Bread Crumbs

As kids, veggies were a regular fixture on the table. But what we'd get really excited for every single time were salads—especially leafy, crunchy salads slathered in a little too much creamy dressing. Caesar salad in particular was always our favorite, which is why we still regularly include it in our lunch and dinner rotation. Except these days we make it with a Mediterranean twist, including using rich, protein-packed tahini in the dressing and finishing things off with pita bread crumbs. It's a fun, fresh update for an old friend.

SERVES 4 TO 6

PITA BREAD CRUMBS

1 (8-inch) day-old pita, roughly torn

¼ cup walnuts

1 tablespoon extra-virgin olive oil

TAHINI-CAESAR DRESSING

½ cup extra-virgin olive oil

½ cup freshly grated parmesan cheese

¼ cup well-stirred tahini

1 tablespoon fresh lime juice

1 medium garlic clove, peeled but whole

2 teaspoons freshly ground black pepper

1 teaspoon anchovy paste, or
2 anchovy fillets finely chopped or
mashed with a fork

½ teaspoon fine sea salt

SALAD

8 cups loosely packed lettuce of your choice (we like romaine, Bibb, or Boston)

1 (15-ounce) can chickpeas, drained and thoroughly rinsed

2 medium avocados, sliced

3 radishes, thinly sliced

¼ cup freshly grated parmesan cheese

Freshly ground black pepper, to taste

MAKE THE PITA BREAD CRUMBS: Preheat the oven to 250°F. Line a sheet pan with foil or parchment paper.

In a food processor, combine the pita, walnuts, and olive oil and pulse until the mixture is coarse and crumbly. Spread the mixture over the prepared sheet pan.

Bake until crispy, 5 to 8 minutes. Set aside to cool while you make the rest of the salad.

MAKE THE TAHINI-CAESAR DRESSING: In a food processor or blender, combine the olive oil, parm, tahini, lime juice, garlic, pepper, anchovy paste, and salt. Process until the dressing is completely smooth.

ASSEMBLE THE SALAD: In a large serving bowl, create a bed of the greens followed by the chickpeas, avocado, and radish slices. Sprinkle with the pita crumbs and drizzle with as much dressing as you prefer (we like using all of it). Finish with the parm and a couple cracks of black pepper, toss, and serve.

MAKE IT AHEAD

You can make the dressing ahead and store in an airtight container for up to 1 week. The pita bread crumbs can be baked and stored in a sealed container at room temperature for up to 1 week.

Lentil Salad with Cumin-Tahini Dressing

FAN
—
FAV

Lentils are a fixture on the Egyptian table, and it's hard not to understand their appeal—they're filling, inexpensive, easy to prepare, and the ultimate blank canvas. While this isn't necessarily a traditional preparation, it feels like something that we could have grown up eating. Between the heaps of crisp raw veg like cucumbers, tomatoes, and bell peppers, handfuls of fresh parsley, and a cumin-scented tahini dressing, it's like a best-of Mediterranean salad. It's also a great one to prep at the beginning of the week and keep in the refrigerator for quick lunches or dinners because it gets even tastier as the lentils and veggies marinate.

SERVES 8

SALAD

2 cups lentils (any variety but red)

1 medium English cucumber, peeled and finely chopped

3 medium Roma tomatoes, finely chopped

1 medium red bell pepper, finely chopped

1 medium orange bell pepper, finely chopped

1 medium green bell pepper, finely chopped

½ medium red onion, finely chopped

½ cup packed finely chopped fresh flat-leaf parsley leaves

Freshly ground black pepper, to taste

CUMIN-TAHINI DRESSING

½ cup extra-virgin olive oil

⅓ cup well-stirred tahini

¼ cup fresh lemon juice (from 1 large lemon)

3 tablespoons distilled white vinegar

1 medium garlic clove, grated

1½ teaspoons fine sea salt, plus more to taste

1½ teaspoons ground cumin

1 teaspoon freshly ground black pepper

MAKE THE SALAD: In a fine-mesh sieve, rinse the lentils under cold water and drain well. Add them to a large pot with 5 cups water and bring to a boil over medium-high heat. Reduce the heat to medium and cook, uncovered, until the lentils are tender, 20 to 25 minutes. Drain and allow the lentils to cool slightly.

In a large serving bowl, combine the cucumber, tomatoes, all the bell peppers, the onion, and parsley and set aside.

MAKE THE CUMIN-TAHINI DRESSING: In a medium bowl or screw-top jar, combine the olive oil, tahini, lemon juice, vinegar, garlic, salt, cumin, and pepper. Whisk or shake vigorously until the dressing is completely smooth and emulsified. Season with more salt, if needed.

To assemble the salad, add the lentils to the bowl with the veggies and drizzle with dressing to taste (we like using all of it). Season with a couple cracks of black pepper, give everything a gentle toss to combine, and coat well in the dressing. Serve now or cover with plastic wrap and refrigerate for 30 minutes for the flavors to meld. Serve chilled or at room temperature.

Store leftovers in an airtight container in the refrigerator for up to 4 days.

Tip for Real Life

If the salad looks a little dry after hanging out in the refrigerator, drizzle with more olive oil and add a squeeze of lemon before serving.

Chickpea-Avocado Salad

This salad is a lot of things to us. First of all, it's delicious, fresh, and filling—everything you want in a salad. But it's actually on repeat in our repertoire because it is a great way to use up that super-ripe avocado on your counter that needs to be eaten stat, plus it gets its protein punch from chickpeas, which are not only inexpensive but are ideal for stockpiling in the pantry. And then there's the fact that it's endlessly versatile. In addition to enjoying it on its own or as a side, it's also great scooped over chicken or fish, as a filling for wraps, or as a condiment for your tacos.

SERVES 4

DRESSING

2 tablespoons fresh lemon juice

2 tablespoons extra-virgin olive oil

2 teaspoons honey

½ teaspoon fine sea salt, plus more to taste

SALAD

1 (15-ounce) can chickpeas, drained and thoroughly rinsed

1 large avocado, diced or sliced

½ cup diced green bell pepper

½ cup packed finely chopped fresh cilantro leaves

1 medium jalapeño pepper, stemmed, seeded (or leave the seeds in if you want more heat), and diced or sliced

1 green onion, both white and green parts, thinly sliced

2 tablespoons finely chopped fresh dill

Freshly ground black pepper, to taste

MAKE THE DRESSING: In a small bowl, whisk together the lemon juice, olive oil, honey, and salt until well combined. Season with more salt, if needed.

ASSEMBLE THE SALAD: In a large bowl, combine the chickpeas, avocado, bell pepper, cilantro, jalapeño, green onion, and dill. Pour in the dressing to taste (we like using all of it). Season with a couple cracks of black pepper and toss until everything is well coated.

MAKE IT AHEAD

Assemble the salad except for the avocado and dressing and store it in an airtight container in the refrigerator for up to 2 days. Add the avocado and dressing just before serving.

Greek Cowgirl Caviar

Cowboy caviar or Texas caviar is a Tex-Mex dish that combines beans, raw veggies, and a vinaigrette-style dressing for a light and simple salad. But we like to imagine that our cowgirl just rode in from Greece, bringing Mediterranean freshness with herbs, Kalamata olives, and a cumin-oregano dressing. This dish could be an appetizer with pita chips or a filling vegetarian main.

SERVES 6 AS A MAIN OR 10 TO 12 AS A STARTER OR SIDE

CUMIN-OREGANO DRESSING

¼ cup extra-virgin olive oil

Juice of 1 large lemon (about ¼ cup)

1 tablespoon honey

1 teaspoon distilled white vinegar

1 teaspoon dried oregano

1 teaspoon ground cumin

1 teaspoon fine sea salt, plus more to taste

½ teaspoon freshly ground black pepper

SALAD

2 (15-ounce) cans chickpeas, drained and thoroughly rinsed

1 (15-ounce) can black beans, drained and thoroughly rinsed

2 cups finely chopped Roma tomatoes (about 4 medium tomatoes)

2 cups finely chopped Persian or English cucumber (about 2 Persian or 1 English)

1 medium red onion, finely chopped

1 cup chopped pitted green olives (we like Manzanilla)

1 cup chopped pitted Kalamata olives

½ cup fresh flat-leaf parsley leaves

½ cup fresh cilantro leaves

MAKE IT AHEAD

Refrigerate the dressing and salad separately in airtight containers for up to 3 days.

MAKE THE CUMIN-OREGANO DRESSING: In a medium bowl, whisk together the olive oil, lemon juice, honey, vinegar, oregano, cumin, salt, and pepper until well combined. Season with more salt, if needed.

ASSEMBLE THE SALAD: In a large bowl, combine the chickpeas, black beans, tomatoes, cucumbers, onion, both olives, parsley, and cilantro. Gently toss to mix well. Drizzle with the dressing to taste (we like using all of it). Gently toss once again to combine.

Make It a Jar

One of our favorite salad hacks is turning meal-prepped salads into grab-and-go jars. Instead of tossing everything together in a container and stashing it in the fridge—which leads to soggy salad and wasted food that nobody wants to eat—we've figured out that you can strategically layer those same components so they stay fresher for longer. These guidelines can be applied to most salads. It's worth noting, however, that not every salad lends itself to this method. To make things easy, we've listed the ones in this chapter that will.

STEP 1: Start with dressing on the bottom; this will keep the salad from getting soggy.

STEP 2: Add any beans or grains (bonus: the beans or grains marinate in some of the dressing!).

STEP 3: Add the veggies.

STEP 4: Add any proteins.

STEP 5: Add your greens.

Store in the refrigerator for up to 5 days.

Salads in this book that would be great as a jar:

Mediterranean Cobb Salad

Give us a salad that's an entire meal chopped up into a bowl, and we couldn't be happier. We especially love a Cobb, with its big chunks of chicken, hard-boiled egg, and crumbles of blue cheese, plus a decadent dressing, so we—obviously—had to put a Middle Eastern/Mediterranean spin on it. You get the same great heartiness, but the layers upon layers of flavor are kicked up a notch with Kalamata olives and a bright, garlicky Dijon vinaigrette. You can't go wrong serving this as a side salad or as the main event.

SERVES 6

DIJON VINAIGRETTE

½ cup extra-virgin olive oil

Juice of 1½ lemons (about ¼ cup)

1 tablespoon Dijon mustard

1 medium garlic clove, minced

1 teaspoon distilled white vinegar

1 teaspoon fine sea salt, plus more
to taste

½ teaspoon freshly ground black pepper

SALAD

1 large or 2 medium heads romaine
lettuce, shredded (about 8 cups)

2 medium Persian cucumbers, sliced, or
½ English cucumber, peeled and sliced

3 hard-boiled eggs (see Tip), sliced

1 (8-ounce) can artichoke hearts, drained
and sliced

1 cup sliced cherry or grape tomatoes

½ medium red onion, thinly sliced

½ cup pitted Kalamata olives

½ cup crumbled blue cheese

Freshly ground black pepper, to taste

MAKE THE DIJON VINAIGRETTE: In a medium bowl, whisk together the olive oil, lemon juice, mustard, garlic, vinegar, salt, and pepper. Season with more salt, if needed.

ASSEMBLE THE SALAD: In a large serving bowl, combine the lettuce, cucumbers, eggs, artichokes, tomatoes, onion, olives, and blue cheese. Drizzle on the dressing to taste (we like using all of it). Season with a couple cracks of black pepper, gently toss until everything is coated well, and serve.

MAKE IT AHEAD

Throw together the dressing, or better yet, a big batch, and store it in an airtight container in the refrigerator for up to 1 week.

Tip for Real Life

Perfect hard-boiled eggs: Bring a medium pot of water to a boil over medium-high heat. Carefully add the eggs, cover, and continue boiling for 9 minutes. Immediately drain the eggs and run them under cold water until they're cool to the touch. Peel and enjoy!

Fattoush with Sumac Vinaigrette

Fattoush indirectly translates in Arabic to "crumb," which is exactly what this Lebanese and Syrian salad is: crumbs, or more accurately, leftover bread. Back in the day, people would take their leftover pita scraps, fry them in oil, then toss them with seasonal vegetables, fresh herbs, plenty of olive oil (obviously), and a good pinch of bright, citrusy sumac. We don't see why we need to improve upon an already really, really good thing, so we're going the traditional route, including making our own sumac-dusted pita chips. That said, we like to bake ours because it means less oil, less splatter, and less hands-on time.

SERVES 6 TO 8

SUMAC-DUSTED PITA CHIPS

2 (8-inch) pitas, cut into 1-inch squares

3 tablespoons extra-virgin olive oil

2 teaspoons ground sumac

½ teaspoon fine sea salt

½ teaspoon freshly ground black pepper

SUMAC VINAIGRETTE

⅓ cup extra-virgin olive oil

Juice of 1½ lemons (about ¼ cup)

1 tablespoon ground sumac

1 tablespoon pomegranate molasses

1 medium garlic clove, grated

1 teaspoon fine sea salt, plus more to taste

SALAD

1 to 2 heads romaine lettuce, sliced crosswise into 1-inch-wide strips (about 6 cups)

2 cups loosely packed fresh flat-leaf parsley leaves, roughly chopped

3 medium Persian or 1 seeded English cucumber, diced

3 medium Roma tomatoes, diced

1 cup loosely packed fresh mint leaves, roughly chopped

½ cup finely chopped green onion, both white and green parts

½ cup thinly sliced radishes (about 5 medium)

Preheat the oven to 375°F.

MAKE THE SUMAC-DUSTED PITA CHIPS: On a sheet pan, combine the pita pieces, olive oil, sumac, salt, and pepper. Toss until the bread is well coated. Spread out the pita in a single layer.

Bake until the chips are crisp and golden, 12 to 15 minutes, tossing about halfway through. Set aside to cool on the pan.

MAKE THE SUMAC VINAIGRETTE: In a medium bowl or screw-top jar, combine the olive oil, lemon juice, sumac, pomegranate molasses, garlic, and salt. Whisk or shake vigorously until the dressing is smooth and emulsified. Season with more salt, if desired.

ASSEMBLE THE SALAD: In a large serving bowl, combine the lettuce, parsley, cucumbers, tomatoes, mint, green onion, and radishes. Add the pita chips and drizzle with the dressing to taste (we like using all of it). Give everything a toss to incorporate well and serve.

MAKE IT AHEAD

The pita chips can be stored in an airtight container at room temperature for up to 1 week. The dressing can be refrigerated in an airtight container for up to 1 week. Hold off on assembling the salad, though, until you're ready to serve in order for it to be as fresh and crunchy as possible.

Egyptian Tomato & Cucumber Salad *(Salata Baladi)*

We like to think of this impossibly simple, juicy, garden-fresh dish as the ultimate Egyptian salad. It's what we're making to serve alongside ful and falafel for breakfast (or brinner!), or as a complement to any Mediterranean–style dinner, especially with grilled meats and fish. And there's basically nothing to it—just tossing together cucumber, tomatoes, onion, and heaps of fresh flat-leaf parsley and mint with an easy drizzle of olive oil and lime juice. Yes, we do call for scooping out the cuke and tomato seeds before chopping them—which ensures maximum crunch and minimum wateriness—but it's 5 minutes well spent.

SERVES 4 TO 6

4 medium Roma tomatoes

4 large Persian cucumbers or
1 peeled English cucumber

½ cup finely chopped red onion
(from ½ medium onion)

½ cup finely chopped fresh mint leaves

½ cup finely chopped fresh flat-leaf
parsley leaves

3 tablespoons extra-virgin olive oil

Juice of 1 lime (about 2 tablespoons)

½ teaspoon fine sea salt, plus more
to taste

Halve the tomatoes lengthwise and use a spoon to gently scoop out the seeds. (You can discard the seeds or use them another time; see Tips.) Dice the tomato "shells" and add them to a large bowl.

Halve the cucumbers lengthwise. If using an English cucumber, use a spoon to gently scoop out the seeds and discard them (or eat them!). Dice the cukes and add them to the bowl with the tomatoes. Add the onion, mint, and parsley and give everything a gentle toss to combine.

In a small bowl, whisk together the olive oil and lime juice. Pour the mixture over the salad and season with the salt. Give the salad another gentle toss until the veggies are well coated. Season with more salt, if needed, and serve.

Store leftovers in an airtight container in the refrigerator for up to 1 day.

MAKE IT AHEAD

Slice all your veggies and store them in an airtight container in the refrigerator overnight. Just hold off on dressing and seasoning them until about 30 minutes before you're ready to serve the salad.

Tips for Real Life

Save those scooped tomato insides! Some ideas for how to use them: Blend for recipes that call for tomato puree; freeze in an ice cube tray and use them for soups or sauces; or use them for homemade salsa.

Reduce the sharpness of the onions by soaking them in cold water for a few minutes. Drain and use as directed.

Cilantro-Cashew Za'atar Salad

Our inspiration for this dish comes from Sweetgreen, a fast casual salad chain, and the days when we treat ourselves to someone else making lunch. Of all the dressing options there, our favorite is the spicy cashew dressing, which makes just about anything taste better. So we gave it a Food Dolls makeover and landed on an equally decadent (and dairy-free) salad topper that's even more vibrant with fresh cilantro and ginger, then added za'atar-sprinkled cashews to the whole mix. It's the kind of salad that you want to dive head-first into, and if we're being really honest with ourselves, is just as convenient as going out (and certainly less expensive).

SERVES 6 TO 8

DRESSING

1 cup loosely packed fresh cilantro leaves

½ cup unsalted cashew butter

¼ cup roughly chopped peeled fresh ginger

2 tablespoons fresh lime juice (from 1 large lime)

2 tablespoons maple syrup

2 tablespoons rice vinegar

2 medium garlic cloves, peeled but whole

1 tablespoon toasted sesame oil

1 tablespoon Aleppo pepper or red pepper flakes (optional), or to taste

½ teaspoon fine sea salt, plus more to taste

SALAD

6 cups shredded green lettuce of your choice (we like romaine)

1 cup shredded red lettuce (or more romaine)

1 cup julienned carrots (from 2 medium carrots)

1 cup thinly sliced Persian or English cucumbers (about 2 medium Persian or ½ peeled English)

2 green onions, both white and green parts, sliced

½ cup roughly chopped salted roasted cashews

2 tablespoons za'atar

MAKE THE DRESSING: In a blender or food processor, combine the cilantro, cashew butter, ginger, lime juice, maple syrup, rice vinegar, garlic, sesame oil, Aleppo (if using), and salt and process until completely smooth. If the dressing is too thick to drizzle, add 1 tablespoon water at a time until you've reached your desired consistency (we like ours thick but pourable). Season with more Aleppo and/or salt, if desired.

ASSEMBLE THE SALAD: In a large serving bowl, combine the green and red lettuces, carrots, cucumber, and green onions. Drizzle with the dressing to taste, sprinkle with the cashews and za'atar, and give everything a gentle toss to mix well.

MAKE IT AHEAD

Refrigerate the dressing in an airtight container for up to 1 week. We like to make a double batch and use it as a dip for chicken strips or as a chicken marinade.

Lentil & Pasta Salad with Spicy Cumin Vinaigrette *(Koshari-ish)*

Koshari is basically the official dish of Egypt. You find it pretty much everywhere—in people's homes, on street food carts—and it's as close to perfect as it gets: warm, hearty, filling, and layered with flavors and textures. But as much as we love our mom's recipe (it will forever be on our best-of lists), we wanted to make a few small tweaks to transform it into an everyday salad. Traditionally, koshari blends lentils and pasta in a cooked tomato sauce with crispy fried onions. We're keeping the must-haves (lentils, pasta, lots and lots of crispy onions), but swapping the sauce for that classic Mediterranean medley of cucumber, tomato, and onion. To bring it all together, we call for a spicy vinaigrette that this salad loves to soak up like a flavor-bomb sponge.

SERVES 6 TO 8

2 cups lentils (any variety but red), soaked in cold water for 30 minutes and drained

1 tablespoon fine sea salt

4 ounces ditalini pasta

SPICY CUMIN VINAIGRETTE

½ cup distilled white vinegar

⅓ cup extra-virgin olive oil

4 medium garlic cloves, grated

2½ teaspoons ground cumin

1½ teaspoons fine sea salt, plus more to taste

1 teaspoon cayenne pepper (optional)

1 teaspoon freshly ground black pepper

SALAD

1½ cups finely chopped tomatoes (about 5 medium Romas)

1½ cups finely chopped Persian or English cucumber (from 3 medium Persian or 1 seeded and peeled medium English cucumber)

1 (15-ounce) can chickpeas, drained and thoroughly rinsed

½ cup diced red onion (from 1 medium onion)

1 cup store-bought crispy onions (we like Trader Joe's), for serving

In a large pot, combine the lentils and 5 cups water. Bring to a boil over medium-high heat, then reduce to a simmer and cook until the lentils are tender, 20 to 25 minutes. Drain and set aside to cool.

Meanwhile, bring a medium pot of water to a boil over medium-high heat. Add the salt and pasta and cook to al dente according to the package directions. Drain and set aside.

MAKE THE SPICY CUMIN VINAIGRETTE: In a medium bowl or screw-top jar, combine the vinegar, olive oil, garlic, cumin, salt, cayenne (if using), and black pepper. Whisk or shake vigorously until the dressing is smooth and emulsified. Adjust the seasoning with more salt, if desired.

ASSEMBLE THE SALAD: In a large bowl, combine the tomatoes, cucumber, chickpeas, and red onion. Add the lentils and pasta and gently toss to combine. Drizzle with the dressing to taste and toss once again to coat everything well. Top with the crispy onions and serve.

Store leftovers in an airtight container in the refrigerator for up to 4 days.

MAKE IT AHEAD

The dressing can be refrigerated in an airtight container for up to 5 days. And you can combine the salad ingredients, excluding the crispy onions, and store them, undressed, in an airtight container in the refrigerator for up to 3 days.

What's *for* Dinner?

The question that launched it all, and the number one reason why we take quick and easy yet deeply flavorful recipes so seriously. We know firsthand what goes into ensuring that every day runs as smoothly as possible: doing laundry, performing errands, managing the activity schedules, checking homework—on top of what you need to do for your job or (gasp) your personal life. Adding "menu coordinator" to your list of responsibilities is no small task, especially because that role comes with the extra pressure of whipping up nourishing meals that everyone at the table will want to eat. We're sweating just thinking about it! Luckily, though, we learned early on from watching our mom how simple cooking techniques plus bold spices and fresh herbs go a long way in adding up to satisfying meals that don't take hours to come together. With a well-stocked pantry and one good grocery shop at the beginning of the week for proteins and produce, it's possible to serve up a steady rotation of dinners that will get the job done.

Spiced Red Lentil Soup *(Shorbet Ads)*

Living in Minnesota requires a go-to stash of comforting soup recipes for the winter months. This is one of our favorites because it brings back memories of Mom's shorbet ads, a creamy lentil soup with the warm glow of golden turmeric and smoky cumin. The lentils lend a hearty body, and a swirl of coconut milk at the end takes it to a velvety, decadent place. We love serving this with crumbled pita chips over the top for a bit of crunch.

SERVES 4 TO 6

SOUP

1 tablespoon unsalted butter

1 tablespoon extra-virgin olive oil

1 large carrot, roughly chopped

2 medium shallots, roughly chopped

4 medium garlic cloves, peeled but whole

2 cups red lentils, drained and thoroughly rinsed

2 teaspoons ground cumin

2 teaspoons smoked paprika

1½ teaspoons fine sea salt, plus more to taste

½ teaspoon freshly ground black pepper, plus more to taste

FOR SERVING

Lemon wedges

Extra-virgin olive oil

Aleppo pepper or red pepper flakes

Fresh cilantro leaves

Homemade Pita Chips (page 85), crushed

MAKE THE SOUP: In a large Dutch oven or soup pot, heat the butter and olive oil over medium heat. When the butter foams, add the carrot, shallots, and garlic and cook, stirring occasionally, until the carrots are lightly browned, about 5 minutes.

Stir in the lentils, cumin, paprika, salt, and pepper and cook, stirring constantly, just until the mixture is fragrant, 1 to 2 minutes. Add 8 cups water and stir to combine. Bring to a boil. Reduce the heat to medium-low, cover, and simmer, stirring occasionally to make sure nothing sticks to the bottom, until the lentils break down, 15 to 20 minutes. Taste and season with more salt and/or pepper, if needed. Remove the pot from the heat.

Use an immersion blender to puree the soup to your desired texture. (Some people like theirs silky smooth; others like it a little chunky.) Alternatively, you could carefully transfer the soup in batches to a stand blender and blend to your desired consistency. Remove the steam vent plug from the blender lid and cover with a thick kitchen towel to prevent any splatter and hold the lid in place while allowing some steam to escape.

TO SERVE: Ladle into bowls and finish with a squeeze of lemon juice, a drizzle of olive oil, a dash of Aleppo, cilantro, and some crushed pita chips.

Store leftovers in the refrigerator for up to 1 week or in the freezer for up to 1 month. Reheat the soup, adjusting the seasoning as needed. The soup can thicken as it sits and cools, so you may also want to add a splash of water or stock to loosen it up.

Tip for Real Life

To make this completely dairy-free, you can use olive oil in place of the butter.

Harissa-Tomato Soup with Halloumi Grilled Cheese

This is our Mediterranean-inspired take on one of the most perfect culinary combos: tomato soup and grilled cheese. As much as we loved our mom's more traditional afternoon snacks, we'd always wish that we could have this classic American pairing on chilly afternoons after school like our friends. So when we got to call our own shots in the kitchen, this was one of the first recipes we wanted to make for our kids. The soup has the same creamy sweetness as the original, but with the added depth of flavor from red bell peppers and spiced harissa paste. And the grilled cheese is the same gooey goodness tomato soup deserves, but with a bright, salty bite from Halloumi (a firm goat and sheep's milk cheese). Make these together for optimal dunking, or make one or the other.

SERVES 4 TO 6

SOUP

8 medium Roma tomatoes, halved

2 medium red bell peppers, quartered

½ medium red onion

1 cup packed fresh basil leaves

4 medium garlic cloves, peeled but whole

3 tablespoons extra-virgin olive oil

2 tablespoons harissa

1 tablespoon tomato paste

1 teaspoon smoked paprika

1 teaspoon dried oregano

1 teaspoon fine sea salt, plus more to taste

½ teaspoon freshly ground black pepper, plus more to taste

FOR SERVING

½ cup heavy cream

Aleppo pepper or red pepper flakes (optional)

Fresh basil leaves

Halloumi Grilled Cheese Sandwiches (recipe follows)

Preheat the oven to 400°F.

MAKE THE SOUP: In a 7 × 11-inch baking dish, combine the tomatoes, bell peppers, onion, basil, garlic, olive oil, harissa, tomato paste, smoked paprika, oregano, salt, and black pepper. Toss everything to evenly coat in the oil and seasonings.

Bake, without stirring, until the vegetables are tender and slightly caramelized 30 to 35 minutes.

Carefully transfer everything from the baking dish, including any juices, to a blender. Remove the steam vent plug from the blender lid and cover with a thick kitchen towel to prevent any splatter and hold the lid in place while allowing some steam to escape. Blend until smooth (pulse a few times first to release some heat). If you'd prefer a thinner soup, you can add a splash of water and blend again until you reach your desired consistency. Season with more salt and/or pepper, if needed.

TO SERVE: Ladle the soup into bowls and finish with a drizzle of heavy cream, a sprinkle of Aleppo (for those who like a little heat), and more fresh basil. Dunk your grilled cheese and enjoy.

Tips for Real Life

Some harissa blends can be spicy—be sure to taste and assess how much heat you want to add to your soup. Feel free to start with less and add more to taste.

If you want a dairy-free option for the soup, use coconut milk instead of the heavy cream.

Halloumi Grilled Cheese Sandwiches MAKES 6 SANDWICHES

You can easily scale this recipe up or down to make more or fewer sandwiches.

- 1 loaf ciabatta (or your favorite) bread cut into twelve 1-inch-thick slices
- 8 ounces Halloumi cheese (see Tips, page 74), cut lengthwise into 6 slices
- Unsalted butter, at room temperature

Top 6 of the bread slices with 1 slice Halloumi each. Place a second slice of bread on top, then spread butter over the outside of each sandwich.

Heat a grill pan or large nonstick skillet over medium heat. Add 1 or 2 sandwiches—depending on the size of your pan—and griddle, gently pressing with a spatula, until the first side is golden brown, 3 to 4 minutes. Flip and griddle the second side, still pressing with a spatula, until it is also golden brown and the cheese is melted (though, it will still be semi-firm), another 3 to 4 minutes. Repeat with any remaining sandwiches. Serve gooey and hot.

Spiced Chickpea & Coconut Stew

We like to observe Meatless Mondays, and when we do, our goal is to find a main dish that is just as filling, satisfying, and delicious as some of our favorite meaty offerings. Our go-to protein source is chickpeas, which have a hearty texture and soak up other flavors like little sponges. When simmered in a flavorful broth scented with some of our favorite spices like smoked paprika and cinnamon, and swirled with rich, velvety coconut milk, they take on a magical life of their own.

SERVES 6 TO 8

2 tablespoons extra-virgin olive oil

1 medium yellow onion, finely chopped

1 medium green bell pepper, chopped

1 medium jalapeño pepper, stemmed, seeded (or leave the seeds in if you want more heat), and diced

4 medium garlic cloves, minced

1 (28-ounce) can whole peeled tomatoes

2 (15-ounce) cans chickpeas, drained and thoroughly rinsed

1 cup low-sodium vegetable stock or water

1½ teaspoons fine sea salt

1 teaspoon sugar

1 teaspoon smoked paprika

½ teaspoon ground cumin

½ teaspoon freshly ground black pepper

¼ teaspoon ground cinnamon

1 cup canned full-fat coconut milk (see Tip)

FOR SERVING

¼ cup finely chopped fresh cilantro leaves

1 lime, cut into wedges

Cooked jasmine or basmati rice, couscous, or pita (optional)

In a large saucepan, heat the olive oil over medium-high heat until it shimmers. Add the onion, bell pepper, jalapeño, and garlic and cook, stirring occasionally, until softened and aromatic, 2 to 3 minutes. Add the tomatoes and their juices, using your spoon to crush them until the mixture is no longer chunky. Stir in the chickpeas, stock, salt, sugar, smoked paprika, cumin, black pepper, and cinnamon. Continue cooking, stirring occasionally, for 25 minutes to reduce the sauce by about one-third and thicken.

Stir in the coconut milk and simmer for 5 more minutes for the flavors to meld. Remove the pot from the heat.

TO SERVE: Ladle the soup into bowls and finish with chopped cilantro and a squeeze of lime juice. Serve with rice, couscous, or pita, if desired.

Store leftovers in an airtight container in the refrigerator for up to 4 days or in the freezer for up to 3 months.

Tip for Real Life

You can use the leftover coconut milk in smoothies or for other soup or sauce recipes. Or you can freeze it for up to 3 months.

Lemony Chicken Soup with Rice

Chicken and rice soup is the universal remedy at our homes for aches, pains, sniffles, and winter blahs. But to give it a sunny Mediterranean twist, we finish ours off with a big squeeze of bright lemon, which not only gives you a healing dose of vitamin C, but also makes all the other flavors come to life.

SERVES 6

1 tablespoon unsalted butter

1 tablespoon extra-virgin olive oil

2 medium carrots, finely chopped

3 celery stalks, finely chopped

½ medium yellow onion, finely chopped

3 medium garlic cloves, minced

2 tablespoons all-purpose flour

8 cups low-sodium chicken broth

3 dried bay leaves

1 teaspoon dried oregano

1 teaspoon fine sea salt, plus more to taste

½ teaspoon dried thyme

½ teaspoon freshly ground black pepper, plus more to taste

1½ pounds boneless, skinless chicken breasts

½ cup uncooked short-grain white rice, thoroughly rinsed until the water runs clear

Juice of 1 lemon (about ¼ cup)

¼ cup finely chopped fresh dill or flat-leaf parsley, for serving

In a large Dutch oven or soup pot, heat the butter and olive oil over medium-high heat. When the butter melts and begins to foam, add the carrots, celery, and onion and sauté, stirring occasionally, until the vegetables are tender, 5 to 7 minutes.

Stir in the garlic and cook, stirring constantly, just until fragrant, about 30 seconds. Add the flour and cook, stirring constantly, until the flour is very lightly browned, about 1 minute. Pour in the broth and stir until the flour has dissolved. Add the bay leaves, oregano, salt, thyme, and pepper and stir to combine.

Add the chicken and rice to the pot and bring to a boil. Reduce the heat to medium-low, cover, and simmer until the chicken is no longer pink inside and the rice is tender, 20 to 25 minutes. Remove the pot from the heat.

Transfer the chicken to a cutting board and slice the breasts into bite-sized pieces. Return them to the pot. Finish the soup with the lemon juice and season with more salt and/or pepper, if needed. Top with dill and serve.

Store leftovers in an airtight container in the refrigerator for up to 3 days.

Med Pizzas with Whipped Ricotta, Arugula & Olives

You *could* get the same-ol', same-ol' pizza delivery. *Or* you could throw together these pita pizzas loaded up with a creamy ricotta spread spiked with salty feta and all the Mediterranean-inspired toppings. The choice is yours!

SERVES 4

WHIPPED RICOTTA

1 (4-ounce) block brine-packed feta cheese

4 ounces cream cheese, at room temperature

⅓ cup whole-milk ricotta cheese

3 fresh basil leaves

Grated zest and juice of ½ lemon (about 1 tablespoon juice)

1 teaspoon dried oregano

PIZZAS

4 (4- to 6-inch) rounds thick Greek pita or naan

4 small Roma tomatoes, sliced

½ cup Kalamata olives, pitted and roughly chopped

½ cup Manzanilla olives, pitted and roughly chopped

2 cups freshly grated low-moisture mozzarella cheese

3 cups baby arugula

⅓ cup freshly grated parmesan cheese

Extra-virgin olive oil, for drizzling

Preheat the oven to 425°F.

MAKE THE WHIPPED RICOTTA: In a food processor or blender, combine the feta, cream cheese, ricotta, basil, lemon zest, lemon juice, and oregano and process until smooth and creamy.

ASSEMBLE THE PIZZAS: Arrange the breads in a single layer on a sheet pan. Divide the ricotta mixture among them and spread it over the entire surface.

Top the ricotta with a few slices of tomato and a scattering of olives. Sprinkle the mozzarella over the top.

Bake until the mozzarella is melted and beginning to brown, 10 to 12 minutes.

Finish each pizza with a handful of arugula, a sprinkle of parm, and a drizzle of olive oil.

Tips for Real Life

You could also make these pizzas on traditional pizza crust using store-bought dough, or use flatbreads or even focaccia.

Add shredded or chopped cooked chicken before sprinkling on the mozzarella for an extra protein boost.

Change up the vegetables: Fresh or roasted options like bell peppers, red onions, baby spinach, and artichokes are all delicious.

Roasted Eggplant with Peppers in Tomato Sauce *(Messaka)*

Egyptian messaka is a distant cousin of the Greek classic, moussaka, an eggplant-centric lasagna-like casserole enveloped in a rich, tomato-y sauce. It's one of those dishes that has as many variations as there are cooks in the kitchen, so in our opinion, there really is no wrong way to messaka, including omitting the beef, which is what we've done here. Instead, we've leaned way into the custardy, caramelized eggplant plus sweet bell peppers, both of which we call for roasting instead of pan-frying because sometimes you need a night off from wiping down your entire stove. It's also a major bonus that it can go directly from skillet to table.

SERVES 4

¼ cup plus 3 tablespoons extra-virgin olive oil

1 teaspoon fine sea salt

¾ teaspoon freshly ground black pepper

2 medium eggplants (2 pounds), sliced into ½-inch-thick rounds

1 medium red bell pepper, cut into 1½-inch squares

1 medium green bell pepper, cut into 1½-inch squares

1 large or 2 small jalapeño peppers, stemmed, seeded (or leave the seeds in if you want more heat), and sliced

3 tablespoons grated garlic (about 6 large cloves)

4 tablespoons tomato paste

2 tablespoons distilled white vinegar

¼ teaspoon sugar

Fresh flat-leaf parsley leaves, for serving

Preheat the oven to 425°F.

In a measuring cup or small bowl, whisk together ¼ cup of the olive oil, ½ teaspoon of the salt, and ¼ teaspoon of the black pepper. Set aside.

Brush a sheet pan with 1 tablespoon of the olive oil. Spread out the eggplants, bell peppers, and jalapeños on the sheet pan and brush the vegetables with the seasoned olive oil mixture.

Roast until the vegetables are beginning to turn golden brown on the edges, 30 to 45 minutes, flipping halfway through. Set aside.

In a large skillet, heat the remaining 2 tablespoons olive oil over medium heat until it shimmers. Add the garlic and sauté, stirring constantly, until just fragrant and beginning to turn lightly golden, 1 to 2 minutes.

Stir in the tomato paste and cook until it just begins to brown, about 2 minutes. Add the vinegar, sugar, the remaining ½ teaspoon of salt, and 1½ cups water and bring to a boil. Reduce the heat to medium and simmer until the flavors meld, 2 to 4 minutes. Fold the roasted eggplant and peppers into the sauce and simmer together until the eggplant softens and the sauce reduces by half, 8 to 10 minutes.

Transfer the dish to a deep serving plate—or serve directly out of the skillet! Sprinkle with parsley before serving.

Store leftovers in an airtight container in the refrigerator for up to 3 days or in the freezer for up to 3 months.

Rice & Herb Stuffed Bell Peppers *(Mahshi Filfil)*

We Middle Easterners love to stuff just about anything—zucchini, tomatoes, grape leaves, cabbage, and of course, bell peppers. The most traditional version of the filling is a rice and beef blend that's fragrant with spices and fresh herbs, but our family's recipe has always been vegetarian because we like serving it as a side with a meat main (especially Mama's Beef Kofta, page 205). While this filling will transform any vegetable vessel into a standout mealworthy dish, we always go for large bell peppers because the prep is the easiest and yet the presentation is effortlessly polished. Just keep in mind that the size of peppers can vary pretty widely, so we call for having 5 to 7 on hand so you don't have to waste any of the precious filling. If you end up with extra bell peppers, use them to dip into Silky-Smooth Hummus (page 94).

SERVES 6 TO 8

SAUCE

2½ cups low-sodium vegetable broth or water

1 cup (8 ounces) canned tomato sauce

½ teaspoon seven spice, store-bought or homemade (page 28)

¾ teaspoon fine sea salt

½ teaspoon freshly ground black pepper

STUFFED PEPPERS

2 cups long-grain rice, such as basmati or jasmine, thoroughly rinsed until the water runs clear and drained

1 cup finely chopped Roma tomatoes (about 2 medium)

1 cup packed finely chopped mixed fresh herbs, such as dill, cilantro, and flat-leaf parsley (we like ⅓ cup of each)

1 medium yellow onion, finely chopped

3 tablespoons tomato paste

3 medium garlic cloves, minced

2 tablespoons extra-virgin olive oil

1½ teaspoons fine sea salt

½ teaspoon freshly ground black pepper

5 to 7 large multicolored bell peppers (yellow, red, and orange are the sweetest)

Fresh dill, for garnish (optional)

Preheat the oven to 350°F.

MAKE THE SAUCE: In a large ovenproof pot or Dutch oven off the heat, stir together the broth, tomato sauce, seven spice, salt, and pepper. Set aside.

MAKE THE STUFFED PEPPERS: In a large bowl, stir together the rice, tomatoes, herbs, onion, tomato paste, garlic, olive oil, salt, and pepper.

Use a sharp knife to slice off the top of each pepper, about ½ inch below the stem. Reserve the tops. Use your fingers or a spoon to gently pull or scoop out the seeds and membranes from inside the peppers, taking care not to tear the peppers. Carefully arrange the peppers in another large pot or Dutch oven so they are standing upright. It's easiest to keep them upright when using a pot that keeps them nice and snug. (We use a 5.5-quart one.) Fill each pepper to the top with the rice mixture and spoon 2 tablespoons of the sauce into each pepper. Place the tops back on the peppers and pour the remaining sauce into the pot around the peppers.

Set the pot over medium-high heat and bring the sauce to a boil. Cover the pot and carefully transfer it to the oven.

Bake until the rice in the filling is tender, 1 hour to 1 hour 10 minutes.

Use a large ladle to carefully transfer the peppers to a serving plate and drizzle over the sauce from the bottom of the pot. Garnish with fresh dill, if desired.

Store leftovers in an airtight container in the refrigerator for up to 4 days.

Tips for Real Life

Look for firm bell peppers with flat bottoms—they'll be easier to stuff and won't spill their contents in the pot! Also, try choosing peppers that are similar in size so they cook evenly.

Cauliflower Steaks with Romesco

It's no secret that cauliflower is one of the most versatile ingredients in the produce crisper, and one of our favorite ways to give it a main-dish moment is by treating it like a tender, juicy steak. By cutting the cauli into slabs and roasting them until caramelized and smoky, you end up with a veg that you can really sink your teeth into. The finishing touch is a slathering of romesco, a deeply savory Spanish tomato and red pepper sauce. You could enjoy this on its own or over a bed of greens or cooked grains (quinoa or farro are both tasty).

SERVES 4

ROASTED CAULIFLOWER

3 tablespoons extra-virgin olive oil

1 teaspoon garlic powder

1 teaspoon fine sea salt

½ teaspoon sweet paprika

½ teaspoon freshly ground black pepper

1 medium head cauliflower, cut lengthwise into ½-inch-thick slices

ROMESCO SAUCE

1 cup cherry tomatoes

1 medium red bell pepper

3 garlic cloves, unpeeled

1 tablespoon sun-dried tomato paste, pureed sun-dried tomatoes, or tomato paste

2 tablespoons extra-virgin olive oil

½ teaspoon fine sea salt, plus more to taste

¼ teaspoon freshly ground black pepper, plus more to taste

¼ cup loosely packed fresh basil leaves, plus more for serving

Parmesan cheese, for serving (optional)

Preheat the oven to 400°F.

ROAST THE CAULIFLOWER: In a small bowl, stir together the olive oil, garlic powder, salt, paprika, and pepper. Arrange the cauliflower slices on a sheet pan in a single layer. Drizzle the olive oil mixture over each slice and use your hands to slather it all over the cauliflower.

Roast until golden and tender, about 30 minutes, flipping the slices about halfway through. (Keep a close eye on these—they like to burn!)

MEANWHILE, MAKE THE ROMESCO SAUCE: In a baking dish large enough to comfortably fit them, combine the tomatoes, bell pepper (left whole), garlic, and tomato paste. Drizzle with the olive oil and season with the salt and pepper.

Roast along with the cauliflower until the vegetables are deeply caramelized, about 30 minutes, flipping halfway through.

When the sauce ingredients are cool enough to handle, peel the garlic and remove the stem and seeds from the bell pepper.

In a blender or food processor, combine the garlic, bell pepper, tomatoes, and any juices from the baking dish along with the basil and blend until the sauce is smooth. Season with salt and pepper, if needed.

To serve, spoon about ¼ cup of the sauce on each of four serving plates. Top the sauce with a cauliflower steak and finish with more basil and parm, if desired.

Store leftover sauce in an airtight container in the refrigerator for up to 1 week.

Tips for Real Life

For an even creamier sauce, add ¼ cup heavy cream or ½ cup whole-milk Greek yogurt when blending.

This sauce is great for all kinds of other uses, such as spooning over pasta, grilled chicken, or roasted vegetable sandwiches.

Stored in the fridge, this sauce will taste delicious all week long, but if you're serving this dish to guests, we recommend making the sauce the day you plan to serve it in order to capture its most vibrant color and flavor.

Pomegranate Molasses Carrots
with Chickpeas & Couscous

Carrots are the unsung heroes of vegetarian mains. Sliced thick and roasted
until their natural sugars caramelize, these get so tender and sweet—they sort
of give yam/sweet potato vibes, but with more to sink your teeth into. And
when you drizzle those carrots plus protein-packed chickpeas with a honey-
pomegranate molasses mix, it creates a tangy-sweet shellac that takes the whole
dish to an even better place. You could stop there and serve it as a side, or heap
it over couscous and have a deeply nourishing meal.

SERVES 4 TO 6

1½ pounds petite (not baby) carrots
(about 12 carrots), halved lengthwise or
quartered, if on the thicker side

1 (15-ounce) can chickpeas, drained and
thoroughly rinsed

¼ cup extra-virgin olive oil

¾ teaspoon fine sea salt

½ teaspoon dried thyme

½ teaspoon freshly ground black pepper

2 tablespoons honey

2 tablespoons pomegranate molasses

8 ounces couscous

FOR SERVING

Salted roasted pistachios

Crumbled feta cheese

Honey, for drizzling

Extra-virgin olive oil, for drizzling

Fresh mint leaves

Preheat the oven to 400°F. Line a sheet pan with foil or parchment paper.

In a large bowl, toss together the carrots, chickpeas, olive oil, salt, and
pepper. Spread everything in a single layer over the prepared pan.

Roast until the carrots are tender and beginning to caramelize, about
20 minutes, stirring or shaking the pan occasionally.

Meanwhile, in a small bowl, stir together the honey and pomegranate
molasses.

Drizzle the honey mixture over the carrots and chickpeas, return to the
oven, and roast, undisturbed, until the carrots are deeply caramelized,
an additional 15 to 20 minutes.

Meanwhile, cook the couscous according to the package directions.

TO SERVE: Spread the couscous over a serving platter and spoon the carrots
and chickpeas over the top, including all the drippings from the pan.
Sprinkle with the pistachios and feta, drizzle with a bit more honey and
olive oil, and finish with mint.

Store leftovers in an airtight container in the refrigerator for up to 3 days.

Veggie-Packed Spaghetti

The name pretty much says it all! But don't be fooled by the straightforward name—this is a hardworking dish. We wanted to develop a meal that not only comes together quickly for busy nights when multiple pots and pans are out of the question, but also delivers maximum veg nutrition (without tasting like it!). The secret is letting everything simmer together in a starchy pasta bath, then adding a lusciously creamy finish with mascarpone and parmesan cheese.

SERVES 6

4 cups low-sodium vegetable broth or water

1 pound spaghetti

2 cups broccoli florets (from 1 medium head)

1 cup roughly chopped zucchini (about 1 small zucchini)

½ cup roughly chopped asparagus (about 5 thin spears)

½ cup frozen green peas

½ small yellow onion, diced

4 medium garlic cloves, minced

2 teaspoons dried oregano

2 teaspoons fine sea salt

1 teaspoon Aleppo pepper or red pepper flakes, or to taste

1 teaspoon sweet paprika

1 teaspoon freshly ground black pepper

½ cup mascarpone cheese

½ cup heavy cream

½ cup packed fresh flat-leaf parsley leaves, finely chopped

1 cup freshly grated parmesan cheese, for serving

In a large Dutch oven or pot, combine the broth, spaghetti, broccoli, zucchini, asparagus, peas, onion, garlic, oregano, salt, Aleppo, paprika, and black pepper. Bring the mixture to a boil over medium-high heat, stirring occasionally. Reduce the heat to medium-low so the pasta is at a low simmer, cover, and cook until the pasta is al dente, 12 to 15 minutes, stirring about halfway through.

Stir in the mascarpone, cream, and parsley and serve topped with plenty of parm.

Store leftovers in an airtight container in the refrigerator for up to 5 days or freeze for up to 3 months.

Tips for One-Pot Pasta Recipes

One-pot pasta recipes are exactly what they sound like: pasta dishes that call for cooking all the ingredients together in a single pot for a super-convenient meal. These recipes are fantastic for busy weeknight dinners, and leftovers always make excellent lunches because these dishes tend to taste even better the next day. But the biggest perk of one-pot pasta recipes is that the noodles soak up all the flavors of the dish, including the sauce and seasonings, instead of just the cooking water.

We have *a lot* of experience with one-pot pastas and have some tried and true tips for success to share:

- Be careful not to overcook the pasta. Aim for al dente since it will continue cooking in the sauce.
- Don't feel like you have to use the type of pasta we call for in the recipe. You can use any long- or short-cut variety.
- You can always adjust the spice by adding more or less of the red pepper flakes.
- Use our one-pot recipes as a jumping-off point—feel free to add proteins such as shrimp, chicken, or ground turkey or beef—which you would cook before adding your veg. Or add sautéed vegetables such as mushrooms, onions, asparagus, broccoli, bell peppers, or spinach.

How to store and reheat:

- Store leftovers in an airtight container in the refrigerator for up to 5 days or freeze for up to 3 months.
- To maintain a smooth sauce consistency when reheating on the stovetop, add a bit of water or broth to the dish. The pasta can be warmed on the stove or in the microwave in intervals, stirring between each.
- For quicker-cooking frozen leftovers, allow them to thaw in the fridge overnight.

Spicy Rigatoni

Sometimes you just need a big bowl of pasta. We get it. But we know we can do a little better than throwing together noodles with store-bought sauce. This recipe requires just as little effort, but with a small handful of additional ingredients, you get a dish that tastes like you spent hours toiling over a spicy marinara. We also love this preparation because you can fold in pretty much any other vegetables, such as raw spinach or sautéed mushrooms, in addition to (or in place of) the peas.

SERVES 6 TO 8

2 tablespoons unsalted butter

5 medium garlic cloves, minced

1 small shallot, diced

2 teaspoons Aleppo pepper or red pepper flakes, or to taste

4 cups low-sodium vegetable broth or water

2½ cups (20 ounces) marinara sauce (we love Rao's)

1 pound rigatoni

1 teaspoon fine sea salt

1 cup frozen green peas

¾ cup heavy cream

½ cup freshly grated parmesan cheese, plus more for serving

Fresh flat-leaf parsley or basil leaves, for serving

In a large Dutch oven or pot, melt 1 tablespoon of the butter over medium-high heat. When the butter just begins to foam, add the garlic, shallot, and Aleppo and sauté, stirring occasionally, until the shallot softens, 1 to 2 minutes.

Add the broth, marinara sauce, rigatoni, and salt and allow the mixture to come to a soft boil. Reduce the heat to medium-low so everything is at a low simmer, cover, and cook until the pasta is al dente, 12 to 13 minutes, stirring once about halfway through.

Stir in the peas, cream, and parm and cook over medium heat until the flavors meld and the sauce is uniform and creamy, 2 to 3 minutes, stirring once midway through. (Be sure to keep things to a very low simmer; you don't want your cream to curdle or separate.) Serve topped with more parm and fresh herbs.

Store leftovers in an airtight container in the refrigerator for up to 3 days.

Greek Pasta with Olives & Feta

This family-favorite takes a traditional red sauce preparation and amps it up with briny olives and salty feta. But the real star is pipe rigate, a small pasta shape that looks like little shells, which cradle the sauce.

SERVES 6 TO 8

2 tablespoons extra-virgin olive oil

½ medium red onion, finely chopped

2 medium garlic cloves, minced

1 tablespoon Greek seasoning, store-bought or homemade (see Tips)

1 cup pitted Manzanilla olives, sliced

1 cup pitted Kalamata olives, sliced

1 cup cherry tomatoes, halved

4 cups low-sodium vegetable broth or water

1 cup (8 ounces) marinara sauce (we love Rao's)

1 pound pipe rigate or other small bite-sized pasta

½ teaspoon fine sea salt, plus more to taste

½ teaspoon freshly ground black pepper

FOR SERVING

Crumbled feta cheese

Finely chopped fresh flat-leaf parsley leaves

Aleppo pepper or red pepper flakes

In a large Dutch oven or pot, heat the olive oil over medium heat. Add the onion and garlic and sauté, stirring occasionally, until the onion turns translucent and aromatic, 3 to 4 minutes. Stir in the Greek seasoning and cook, stirring, for about a minute to infuse the flavors.

Add both olives and the tomatoes and cook, stirring occasionally, until the tomatoes begin to soften, about 2 minutes. Stir in the broth, marinara, pasta, salt, and black pepper and allow the mixture to come to a boil over medium-high heat. Reduce the heat to medium-low so everything is at a low simmer, cover, and cook, stirring occasionally, until the pasta is al dente, 11 to 13 minutes. Adjust the seasoning with more salt, if needed.

Serve sprinkled with feta, parsley, and Aleppo.

Store leftovers in an airtight container in the refrigerator for up to 5 days. When reheating leftovers, you may want to add a splash of broth or water to loosen up the sauce. The pasta likes to soak it up as it cools.

Tips for Real Life

Homemade Greek seasoning: You could use a store-bought Greek seasoning blend or make your own with 2 teaspoons onion powder, 2 teaspoons garlic powder, 2 teaspoons dried oregano, 2 teaspoons dried basil, 1 teaspoon dried dill, 1 teaspoon dried thyme, 1 teaspoon fine sea salt, and 1 teaspoon freshly ground black pepper. Store any leftover in an airtight container in your spice cabinet for up to 1 year.

For even more heat, you can add a pinch of red pepper flakes when you're sautéing the onion and garlic.

If you're not a fan of olives, you can swap them out for artichoke hearts or capers.

Parmesan-Crusted Tilapia with Mango Avocado Salsa

One of our favorite types of fish to cook is tilapia, a white freshwater fish that's extremely versatile both in flavor and how it likes to be prepared, whether it's pan-fried or baked. To us, there's nothing more exciting to sit down to than a piece of fish with a gorgeous golden crust and a moist, flaky center, which we've perfected thanks to a combination of a double dredge, meaning it gets coated in smoky parmesan-panko twice, equaling double the crunchy coating. The only thing better than enjoying this fish as is over rice or grilled veg is piling it high with a fresh, light mango and avocado salsa.

SERVES 4

MANGO AVOCADO SALSA

2 medium mangoes, diced

1 medium avocado, diced

1 small red onion, minced (about ¼ cup)

¼ cup minced fresh cilantro leaves

1 medium jalapeño pepper (optional), stemmed, seeded (or leave the seeds in if you want more heat), and minced

2 tablespoons fresh lime juice (from 1 large lime)

2 teaspoons honey

Fine sea salt

PARMESAN-CRUSTED TILAPIA

4 tilapia fillets (about 5 ounces each)

1½ cups panko bread crumbs

½ cup freshly grated parmesan cheese

2 tablespoons chile powder

1 tablespoon sweet paprika

2 teaspoons garlic powder

2 teaspoons fine sea salt

¾ teaspoon freshly ground black pepper

3 large eggs

¾ cup all-purpose flour

2 tablespoons neutral high-heat oil, such as avocado or vegetable

Lemon or lime wedges, for squeezing

Cooked jasmine rice (optional), for serving

MAKE THE MANGO AVOCADO SALSA: In a medium bowl, stir together the mangoes, avocado, onion, cilantro, and jalapeño (if using). Drizzle the lime juice and honey over the mixture, season with a pinch of salt, and gently toss the ingredients until everything is well coated. Season with more salt, if needed. Cover the bowl with plastic wrap and place it in the refrigerator while you make the tilapia.

PREPARE THE PARMESAN-CRUSTED TILAPIA: Pat dry the fish with paper towels. (Don't skip this step; it'll help you get a crispier crust!)

Set up a dredging station in three shallow bowls: In one bowl, stir together the panko, parm, chile powder, paprika, garlic powder, 1 teaspoon of the salt, and ½ teaspoon of the black pepper. In a second bowl, whisk the eggs with ½ teaspoon of the salt and the remaining ¼ teaspoon black pepper. In a third bowl, combine the flour with the remaining ½ teaspoon salt.

Working with one fillet at a time, coat the tilapia in the eggs, allowing any excess to drip off. Dredge the tilapia in the flour, followed by another round of egg. Finally dredge it in the panko mixture, pressing it into the fish to help it adhere. You want the fish to be evenly and completely coated.

Line a plate with paper towels. In a large skillet, heat the oil over medium-high heat until it shimmers. Working in batches to avoid crowding the pan, carefully add the fish and cook until crispy and golden on the first side, 3 to 4 minutes. Flip and repeat on the second side until crispy and golden and the fish is opaque and flakes easily, another 3 to 4 minutes. Transfer the fish to the paper towels.

To serve, arrange the fish on a plate and top with the salsa. Give everything a squeeze of lemon and serve as is or with rice, if desired.

Store leftover fish in an airtight container in the refrigerator for up to 3 days. Reheat the tilapia in the oven or toaster oven to maintain its crispiness. We recommend making the salsa fresh if you want to enjoy it again.

Tips for Real Life

Make sure the mangoes are ripe; you want them sweet and juicy for this salsa.

We love this salsa with classic cilantro, but try it with mint or basil for a twist.

If you can only find frozen tilapia, that's okay! Most "fresh" fish that you see at the grocery store has already been frozen. Just be sure to really remove any excess moisture from thawed frozen fish.

Air-fry it: Preheat an air fryer to 375°F. Working in batches, arrange the coated tilapia fillets in the air fryer basket in a single layer and air-fry for 10 to 12 minutes, flipping about halfway through, until the fish is crispy and golden brown and cooked through.

Tip for Real Life

A mandoline is not only going to get you a nice, thin slice on your cabbage (essential for optimal slaw texture), but it's also going to save you SO much time.

Spicy Aleppo Shrimp Tacos with Creamy Tahini Slaw

Shrimp is already at the top of our list for quick meals that feel so much fancier than they are, but bundling them up into tacos makes it a next-level favorite. Here, we toss the shrimp with a simple spice blend that gets a punch of citrus from sumac and a spicy kick from Aleppo pepper, quickly pan-sear it, pile it into tortillas, then top it off with a nutty, creamy slaw. There's not a summer spread or barbecue menu that wouldn't benefit from this dish.

SERVES 4 (MAKES 8 TACOS)

CREAMY TAHINI SLAW

½ cup sour cream

3 tablespoons fresh lime juice (from about 2 limes)

2 tablespoons well-stirred tahini

2 medium garlic cloves, minced

1 teaspoon fine sea salt

½ teaspoon freshly ground black pepper

½ head green cabbage (about 1 pound), thinly sliced (see Tip)

1 cup packed fresh cilantro leaves, finely chopped

ALEPPO SHRIMP

1 pound large shrimp (21/25 count), peeled and deveined (see sidebar), tails off

1 teaspoon ground sumac

1 teaspoon Aleppo pepper

½ teaspoon freshly ground black pepper

½ teaspoon fine sea salt

2 tablespoons extra-virgin olive oil

ASSEMBLY

8 (8-inch) corn-flour blend tortillas (or your favorite tortillas)

Finely chopped cilantro leaves

Ground sumac and/or Aleppo pepper

Hot sauce (optional)

MAKE THE CREAMY TAHINI SLAW: In a large bowl, whisk together the sour cream, lime juice, tahini, garlic, salt, black pepper, and ¼ cup water until smooth. Add the cabbage and toss thoroughly to coat. Fold in the cilantro until it is evenly distributed. Set aside.

COOK THE ALEPPO SHRIMP: In a large bowl, combine the shrimp, sumac, Aleppo, salt, and black pepper. Toss together until the shrimp are evenly coated with the spices.

In a large skillet, heat the olive oil over medium heat until it shimmers. Add the shrimp in a single layer and cook until the first side is lightly golden and opaque, 2 to 3 minutes. (You may need to do this in batches.) Flip and repeat on the other side, until the flesh is completely pink and opaque, another 1 to 2 minutes. Remove the pan from the heat.

ASSEMBLE THE TACOS: Warm the tortillas directly over the flame of a stove burner until charred, about 30 seconds per side. Or you can do this on a baking sheet under the broiler for 1 to 2 minutes.

Place three shrimp in each tortilla and top with about ⅓ cup of the slaw. Finish with a sprinkle of cilantro and sumac and/or Aleppo and hot sauce, if desired.

Store leftover shrimp and slaw in separate sealed containers in the refrigerator for up to 3 days.

How to Devein Shrimp

You can leave the shell on or off, depending on your preference. If you're leaving the shell on, use a pair of kitchen shears or a sharp knife to cut through the shell along the back of the shrimp. If you're removing the shell, gently peel it away starting from the underside of the shrimp. Lay the shrimp on a cutting board with its back facing up. Look for the vein: It should be visible as a dark line running along the back of the shrimp. Use the tip of the knife or your fingers to lift the vein out of the shrimp. You can use a paper towel to grab hold of it if it's slippery. After removing the vein, rinse the shrimp under cold water to remove any remaining debris.

Shrimp Tagine with Garlicky Tomatoes & Peppers

This cozy dish has been handed down through the generations of our family, from our grandmother to our mother and then on to us. While tagine is a classic Middle Eastern preparation—named after the type of pot used to stew together an aromatic blend of vegetables, meats, and spices—it's not as common to see seafood in the mix. But our grandma Aliyah, or Teita, which is what we called her ("grandma" in Arabic), was originally from Damietta, a city in northeast Egypt along the Mediterranean coast where fresh fish and shellfish were widely available. We love how light this meal is, yet the combination of jammy tomatoes and peppers—plus many, many memories of this simmering on the stove at Teita's house—makes it feel like a warm hug.

SERVES 4

2 tablespoons extra-virgin olive oil

2 small shallots, sliced

3 medium garlic cloves, grated

2 medium Roma tomatoes, finely chopped

½ cup canned tomato sauce

1 teaspoon fine sea salt

1 teaspoon ground cumin

½ teaspoon smoked paprika

½ teaspoon freshly ground black pepper

½ cup finely chopped red bell pepper (from 1 small pepper)

1 small jalapeño pepper (optional), stemmed, seeded (for less heat), and finely chopped

1 pound large shrimp (21/25 count), peeled and deveined (see page 179)

½ cup finely chopped fresh flat-leaf parsley leaves

Preheat the oven to 400°F.

In a large skillet, heat the olive oil over medium-high heat. When the oil shimmers, add the shallots and sauté, stirring occasionally, until they begin to soften, 3 to 4 minutes. Add the garlic and sauté, stirring frequently, just until fragrant, about another minute.

Add the tomatoes and cook, stirring often, until they start to break down, 3 to 4 minutes. Stir in the tomato sauce, salt, cumin, smoked paprika, black pepper, and 1 cup water and allow the mixture to come to a simmer. Add the bell peppers and jalapeño (if using) and continue simmering, stirring occasionally, until the peppers are tender and the sauce has reduced by one-third, about 10 minutes. Fold in the shrimp and about half of the parsley and remove the pan from the heat.

Transfer the mixture to a 2-quart tagine or large ovenproof dish (we use our 7 × 11-inch baking dish). Carefully transfer it to the oven and bake until the shrimp are pink and opaque, about 10 minutes.

Sprinkle with the remaining parsley and serve.

Store leftovers in an airtight container in the refrigerator for up to 2 days. Be sure to gently reheat the stew to avoid overcooking the shrimp.

Tip for Real Life

You could substitute white fish, such as tilapia or cod, for the shrimp. Increase the cook time to 12 to 14 minutes; the fish should be opaque and flaky.

Sumac Salmon Bowls with Tomato-Cucumber Salad & Avocado Mash

A request we get all the time is for recipes that give people the confidence to cook fish well at home. This technique for cooking salmon pretty much guarantees moist, flaky fish every time. And to keep things interesting, we're spicing it up with bright sumac plus a surprising drizzle of honey. You could serve this salmon with your favorite veg side and rice, or you could toss together a quick marinated tomato and cucumber salad and add a dollop of avocado mash.

SERVES 4

TOMATO-CUCUMBER SALAD

5 medium Persian cucumbers

1½ cups cherry tomatoes

1 tablespoon extra-virgin olive oil

1 teaspoon distilled white vinegar

Fine sea salt and freshly ground black pepper

AVOCADO MASH

2 medium avocados, halved and pitted

Juice of 1 lime (about 2 tablespoons)

½ teaspoon fine sea salt

½ teaspoon freshly ground black pepper

SUMAC SALMON

1 teaspoon ground sumac, plus more for serving

1 teaspoon fine sea salt

½ teaspoon garlic powder

½ teaspoon onion powder

½ teaspoon dried thyme

½ teaspoon dried oregano

¼ teaspoon freshly ground black pepper, plus more for serving

1 pound salmon fillets, skinned, pin bones removed (ask your fishmonger to do this)

1 tablespoon unsalted butter

2 teaspoons honey

Flaky sea salt, for serving

MAKE THE TOMATO-CUCUMBER SALAD: Slice the cucumbers into 1/4-inch-thick coins and halve the cherry tomatoes. In a medium bowl, toss together the cucumbers and cherry tomatoes. Add the oil and vinegar and season with a good pinch of salt and a couple cracks of black pepper. Fold everything together until the veggies are well coated. Set aside to marinate at room temperature while you make the avocado mash and salmon.

MAKE THE AVOCADO MASH: Scoop the avocado flesh into a medium bowl. Use a fork to mash the avocado to your liking. (We leave ours a little chunky.) Add the lime juice, salt, and pepper and stir to combine. Set aside.

MAKE THE SUMAC SALMON: Cut the salmon into 2-inch cubes. In a large bowl, stir together the sumac, salt, garlic powder, onion powder, thyme, oregano, and pepper. Add the salmon and toss to coat each piece with the spice rub.

In a large skillet, melt the butter over medium heat. When the butter begins to foam, add the salmon and cook until the flesh is opaque and flakes easily, 3 to 4 minutes per side. Remove the pan from the heat and drizzle the salmon with the honey.

Divide the salad and all the juices that have collected in the bowl among four serving bowls. Mound the salmon on top, followed by a dollop of the avocado mash and a sprinkle of flaky salt, pepper, and sumac.

Tips for Real Life

Preparing the salad first allows it to develop more flavor while you prepare the other components. You could make it up to 3 days ahead, but leave out the salt until just before serving or it will draw out too much liquid.

You can keep this salad simple, as we have here, or really doll it up by adding crisp sliced veg such as radishes, red onions, or bell peppers; or folding in cubes of feta cheese.

Creamy Lemon-Sumac Linguine & Shrimp

We can't decide what we love more: the fact that this dish is bursting with the sunny combination of sumac and lemon, or that it completely transforms two of our go-to kitchen essentials, shrimp and linguine. And then there's the minor detail that it comes together in a handful of minutes, yet tastes anything but casual. This is frequently on the table for weeknight dinners, but it's also one of those great meals that you can easily dress up for company or special occasions, especially when you accessorize it with our Tahini Caesar (page 133).

SERVES 4 TO 6

Fine sea salt

SHRIMP

1 teaspoon ground sumac

1 teaspoon fine sea salt

½ teaspoon dried oregano

½ teaspoon freshly ground black pepper

1 pound large shrimp (21/25 count), peeled and deveined (see page 179), tails off

1 tablespoon extra-virgin olive oil

LINGUINE

1 pound linguine

1 tablespoon unsalted butter

1 tablespoon extra-virgin olive oil

3 medium garlic cloves, grated

Grated zest and juice of 1 lemon (about ¼ cup)

1 teaspoon Aleppo pepper or red pepper flakes

1 cup heavy cream

1 teaspoon fine sea salt

½ teaspoon freshly ground black pepper

½ cup freshly grated parmesan cheese, plus more for serving

Finely chopped fresh flat-leaf parsley leaves, for serving

Bring a large pot of salted water to a boil over medium-high heat.

MEANWHILE, PREPARE THE SHRIMP: In a large bowl, stir together the sumac, salt, oregano, and black pepper. Add the shrimp and give them a good toss to ensure an even coating of the seasonings. Allow the shrimp to sit for 5 minutes to absorb the flavors.

In a large skillet, heat the olive oil over medium-high heat until it shimmers. Add the shrimp in a single layer without crowding the pan. (You may need to do this in batches.) Cook until the shrimp are beginning to curl, 2 to 3 minutes. Flip and cook until the shrimp are firm and opaque, another 1 to 2 minutes. Transfer the shrimp to a plate and set aside (don't clean the skillet—you'll use it again).

MAKE THE LINGUINE: Add the linguine to the boiling water and cook to al dente according to the package directions. Reserving ½ cup of the cooking water, drain the pasta.

Meanwhile, in the same skillet you used to cook the shrimp, melt the butter with the olive oil over medium heat. Once the butter is melted, add the garlic, lemon zest, and Aleppo. Sauté while stirring until fragrant, about 1 minute.

Add the lemon juice and allow it to reduce by about half, 2 to 3 minutes. Stir in the cream and season with the salt and black pepper. Allow the sauce to gently simmer until the sauce has thickened and the flavors have melded, 2 to 3 minutes. (Take care to keep the sauce at a gentle simmer or the cream will curdle.)

Remove the pan from the heat and fold in the parm until the sauce is creamy and smooth. (Doing this off the heat helps prevent the cheese from clumping up.)

Add the pasta to the sauce and stir to coat well. To help the sauce cling to the noodles or to thin it out, add some of the reserved cooking water a couple tablespoons at a time until you've reached your desired consistency. Toss the cooked shrimp with the pasta and finish with parsley and more parm. Serve hot.

Tips for Real Life

When making the cream sauce, be patient! Allowing the lemon juice to reduce before adding the cream intensifies the lemon flavor in the dish.

Get creative: Go wild with veg—halved cherry tomatoes, broccoli, and asparagus would all be delicious sautéed with the garlic until tender, or you could fold in a few handfuls of baby spinach or arugula with the shrimp. The residual heat will wilt them down.

If you like more heat, add more red pepper flakes to the sauce. Taste as you go and remember: You can always add more, but you can't take any away!

We love serving this dish in a wide, shallow bowl so you can really see the pasta studded with the beautiful shrimp.

Saucy Spiced Chicken Legs & Potatoes

This dish is all about the power of the marinade: a creamy yogurt-based mixture that's loaded with garlic, spices, and a little pomegranate molasses for a tangy pop of flavor. Then the chicken legs are roasted over potatoes, which soak up all the savory juices while crisping in the oven. Yes, this one takes some time to marinate and roast, but it's almost all hands-off—until it's time to dig in.

SERVES 6

SPICE MIX

2 teaspoons fine sea salt

1 teaspoon garlic powder

1 teaspoon onion powder

1 teaspoon ground coriander

1 teaspoon ground sumac

1 teaspoon ground turmeric

1 teaspoon smoked paprika

1 teaspoon freshly ground black pepper

MARINADE

1 cup packed fresh cilantro leaves

1 cup roughly chopped green onion, both white and green parts (about 3 onions)

1 small red onion, roughly chopped

1 large Roma tomato, roughly chopped

½ medium red bell pepper

5 medium garlic cloves, peeled but whole

¼ cup extra-virgin olive oil

¼ cup whole-milk plain yogurt

¼ cup tomato paste

1 medium jalapeño pepper, stemmed and seeded (for less heat)

Juice of 1 lime (about 2 tablespoons)

1 tablespoon pomegranate molasses

CHICKEN AND POTATOES

6 bone-in, skin-on chicken leg quarters

2 pounds baby Yukon Gold potatoes, halved

Chopped scallions, for garnish

MAKE THE SPICE MIX: In a bowl, stir together the salt, garlic powder, onion powder, coriander, sumac, turmeric, paprika, and black pepper.

MAKE THE MARINADE: In a food processor or blender, combine the cilantro, green onion, red onion, tomato, bell pepper, garlic, olive oil, yogurt, tomato paste, jalapeño, lime juice, pomegranate molasses, and spice mix and process until smooth.

PREPARE THE CHICKEN: Use the tip of a sharp knife to score the chicken legs two to three times on each side, about ¾ inch deep and each 1 inch apart (this helps the chicken soak up all that flavor in the marinade). Add the chicken to a large bowl or baking dish and pour half of the marinade over the top. Give everything a good toss to make sure the chicken is well coated. Cover with plastic wrap and transfer to the refrigerator to marinate for at least 30 minutes or up to overnight. (The longer it goes, the more flavor it will have.) Cover and refrigerate the remaining marinade.

When ready to cook, preheat the oven to 425°F.

Arrange the potatoes in a single layer in a 9 × 13-inch baking dish. Mix the potatoes with the remaining marinade, giving them a toss to ensure they're well coated. Place the chicken on top of the potatoes and cover with parchment paper, followed by a tightly crimped layer of foil. (The double layer helps the chicken retain moisture and keeps any flavor from "escaping.")

Roast for 45 minutes. Remove the parchment and foil and roast until the potatoes are tender and the chicken is golden and an instant-read thermometer inserted in the thickest part reads 165°F, an additional 15 minutes. For an extra-crispy finish, switch the oven to broil and hit the chicken and potatoes with that heat until the chicken is golden and crisp, about 5 minutes if on the bottom rack, 2 to 3 minutes if on the upper.

Sprinkle with the scallions and serve.

"Already Taken" Chicken

A version of this recipe went viral on TikTok when it was anointed "Marry Me Chicken," as in, your partner wouldn't be able to resist proposing after being treated to this dish. We're never going to pass up the opportunity to make chicken breasts luxuriating in a creamy tomato-y Jacuzzi, so we made a few Mediterranean-inspired tweaks, such as packing this full of greens and sun-dried tomatoes. We decided that it was so much better than the original that there was no way there wasn't already a ring on it! You're not only guaranteed perfectly tender, juicy chicken, but the whole thing takes less than 30 minutes to make.

SERVES 4

1½ pounds boneless, skinless chicken breasts (2 large)

⅓ cup all-purpose flour

1 teaspoon dried thyme

1 teaspoon dried oregano

½ teaspoon sweet paprika

½ teaspoon fine sea salt, plus more to taste

½ teaspoon freshly ground black pepper, plus more to taste

4 tablespoons extra-virgin olive oil

1 pound cremini mushrooms, sliced

½ cup oil-packed sun-dried tomatoes, drained

3 medium garlic cloves, minced

1 teaspoon Aleppo pepper or red pepper flakes

½ cup heavy cream

½ cup low-sodium chicken broth

3 cups packed baby spinach

1 cup freshly grated parmesan cheese

Carefully use a sharp knife to slice the chicken breasts parallel to the cutting board through the middle to create two thinner halves. Line a clean work surface with parchment paper and lay the chicken pieces on top (you may need to work in batches). Cover the chicken with another piece of parchment and use a meat mallet, rolling pin, or the bottom of a small skillet to pound the chicken to an even ¼-inch thickness.

In a shallow bowl, stir together the flour, thyme, oregano, paprika, salt, and black pepper. Season the chicken with more salt and black pepper, then dredge the chicken through the flour mixture, ensuring it's evenly coated. Shake off any excess flour.

In a large nonstick skillet, heat 2 tablespoons of the olive oil over medium heat until it shimmers. Add the chicken and allow the first side to sear until golden, 3 to 5 minutes. Flip and sear the other side until golden, another 3 to 5 minutes. You don't need (or want) the chicken to be cooked through at this point! Transfer the chicken to a plate and set aside.

Add the remaining 2 tablespoons olive oil to the skillet, along with the mushrooms, sun-dried tomatoes, garlic, and Aleppo. Cook, stirring frequently to avoid burning, until the garlic is fragrant, 3 to 5 minutes.

Stir in the cream and broth, using a wooden spoon to scrape up any browned bits from the bottom of the pan. Add the spinach and parm and allow the spinach to wilt, 1 to 2 minutes, before returning the chicken to the pan. Spoon some sauce over the chicken and cook, uncovered, until the chicken is no longer pink in the center, 3 to 4 minutes.

Remove the pan from the heat and serve.

Store leftovers in an airtight container in the refrigerator for up to 4 days.

Tips for Real Life

You can use boneless, skinless chicken thighs in place of the breasts, but be aware that they will take longer to cook.

You can really pack this dish full of veg. Try adding any of your favorite tender veggies such as asparagus, peas, or cauliflower. Sauté the chopped vegetables with or in place of the mushrooms until just shy of being tender, then proceed with the recipe.

Sumac-Spiced Whole Chicken & Onions with Pitas

Sumac onions (raw onions marinated in vinegar and a warm medley of spices) is one of our favorite condiments that we consistently count on to make any savory dish even better. We wanted to take that same umami-rich flavor profile and feature it as part of a main dish, so here we're roasting the onions, but not before layering a butterflied chicken over the top to baste everything with its juices. Served over pita to sop up every golden drop, this is one of those dishes that you can easily throw together on a weeknight but would also wow a crowd.

SERVES 6

¼ cup extra-virgin olive oil

3 tablespoons fresh lemon juice

3 tablespoons ground sumac

2 teaspoons fine sea salt

1 teaspoon ground cumin

1 teaspoon freshly ground black pepper

¼ teaspoon ground allspice

¼ teaspoon ground cinnamon

2 large red onions, halved and thinly sliced (about 2⅔ cups)

1 whole chicken (3 to 4 pounds)

1 lemon, cut into wedges

¼ cup roughly chopped fresh flat-leaf parsley leaves, for serving

6 (8-inch) pitas, for serving

Tip for Real Life

While we have faith that you can butterfly a chicken, if you're feeling nervous, you can ask your butcher to do it for you.

Preheat the oven to 350°F. Line a sheet pan with foil or parchment paper.

In a small bowl, stir together the olive oil, lemon juice, sumac, salt, cumin, pepper, allspice, and cinnamon.

Add the onions to the sheet pan and drizzle them with 2 tablespoons of the sumac mixture. Give the onions a toss until they are well coated, then spread them into a single layer. Set aside.

Now we're going to butterfly the chicken—it's okay, you got this! Place the bird breast-side down on a clean work surface. Use kitchen shears or a sharp knife to cut along one side of the backbone from tail to neck. Repeat this on the other side of the backbone, then remove it completely. (You can discard it or throw it in a bag in the freezer with your chicken carcass and make stock.) Open the chicken like a book and press down firmly on the breastbone to flatten it. You may hear some popping noises—disregard and think of the delicious roast chicken you're about to eat.

Gently lift the skin from the breast on one side and spoon a little of the marinade inside. Do the same on the other breast. Rub the remaining marinade over every nook and cranny of the chicken, including the underside.

Set a cooling rack on top of the onion mixture in the sheet pan and place the chicken on the rack. Roast for 60 to 70 minutes, until an instant-read thermometer inserted in the thigh registers 165°F.

Transfer the chicken to a platter and allow it to rest at room temperature for 15 minutes before slicing.

To serve, carve the breasts from the chicken and slice. Remove the legs and separate the drumsticks and thighs. Lay the chicken pieces on a platter, followed by the sumac onions. Squeeze on lemon juice, sprinkle with parsley, and serve with the pita bread.

Creamy Chicken Spaghetti Bake *(Negresco)*

This traditional Egyptian casserole is essentially a cross between mac 'n' cheese and chicken noodle soup, which pretty much just means that it's the winner of comfort food everywhere. No one really knows how noodles baked in a béchamel sauce made its way to Egypt or whether we have the Italians or the Greeks to credit, but to whoever is responsible, all we can say is *thank you*.

SERVES 6 TO 8

1 tablespoon plus 1 teaspoon fine sea salt

1 pound spaghetti

Softened butter, for the baking dish

8 tablespoons (1 stick/4 ounces) unsalted butter

½ cup all-purpose flour

4 cups whole milk

2½ cups low-sodium chicken stock

1 dried bay leaf

¾ teaspoon garlic powder

¾ teaspoon freshly ground black pepper

⅛ teaspoon ground nutmeg

⅔ cup freshly grated parmesan cheese

4 cups shredded rotisserie or leftover roasted chicken (white meat, dark meat, or a mix of both)

1½ cups shredded low-moisture mozzarella cheese

Bring a large pot of water to a boil over medium-high heat. Add 1 tablespoon of the salt and the spaghetti and cook for 2 minutes less than the package directions for al dente. Drain and set aside.

Preheat the oven to 400°F. Grease a 9 × 13-inch baking dish with butter.

In a medium saucepan, melt the 8 tablespoons butter over medium heat. When the butter begins to foam, whisk in the flour. Continue whisking constantly for another minute or two, just to eliminate the raw flour taste. Still whisking, gradually add the milk, stock, bay leaf, remaining 1 teaspoon salt, the garlic powder, pepper, and nutmeg. Increase the heat to medium-high and continue whisking as the mixture comes to a boil. Reduce the heat to medium-low and allow the mixture to simmer until it is thick and creamy, 2 to 3 minutes. Remove the pot from the heat, discard the bay leaf, and stir in the parm.

Measure out 3 cups of the sauce and set aside. Add the cooked spaghetti and shredded chicken to the pot with the remaining sauce and stir to coat well. Transfer the mixture to the prepared baking dish and use the back of a spoon to spread it evenly. Pour the reserved sauce over the top of the casserole and sprinkle with the mozzarella.

Bake until the top is golden brown and bubbling, 15 to 20 minutes. You'll want to keep a close eye on things to ensure the casserole doesn't burn.

Allow the casserole to cool for 15 minutes before slicing it into squares—which, yes, will lose their shape and that's okay!—and serving.

MAKE IT AHEAD

You can assemble the casserole a day in advance, cover with plastic wrap, and refrigerate. Then bake when you're ready to serve. Just be sure to add a few more minutes to the baking time if it's cold from the fridge.

Tips for Real Life

Be careful not to overcook your pasta or it will get mushy as it bakes. It should have a little bite to it.

You could make this dish with linguine or short-cut pastas such as penne.

This is a great dish for folding in a variety of cooked veg: Sautéed mushrooms, peas, bell peppers, and spinach would all work here.

Sun-Dried Tomato & Arugula Pasta with Herbed Chicken

And now for one of our favorite creations: a chicken and pasta dish that comes together in a single pot. It's a major Med-vibe moment with Italian-herbed chicken, savory sun-dried tomatoes, artichokes (don't worry—we use jarred ones!), and peppery arugula, plus a little extra decadence from a drizzle of heavy cream. But we mostly love it because it's your main, your side, and your veg all bundled into one delicious dish.

SERVES 6

HERBED CHICKEN

2 pounds boneless, skinless chicken breasts or cutlets

1½ tablespoons Italian seasoning

1 teaspoon fine sea salt

1 teaspoon garlic powder

1 teaspoon onion powder

½ teaspoon freshly ground black pepper

2 tablespoons extra-virgin olive oil

PASTA

2 tablespoons oil from a jar of sun-dried tomatoes

1 cup finely chopped oil-packed sun-dried tomatoes, drained

1 small yellow onion, diced

4 medium garlic cloves, minced

1 teaspoon Italian seasoning

4 cups low-sodium chicken broth

1 pound medium pasta shells

8 ounces baby arugula or baby spinach

1 cup freshly grated parmesan cheese, plus more for serving

¾ cup heavy cream

½ cup chopped marinated artichoke hearts (half a 10-ounce jar)

MAKE THE HERBED CHICKEN: If using chicken breasts (as opposed to cutlets), carefully use a sharp knife to slice the chicken parallel to the cutting board through the middle to create two thinner halves. Line a clean work surface with parchment paper and lay the chicken pieces on top (you may need to work in batches). Cover the chicken with another piece of parchment and use a meat mallet, rolling pin, or the bottom of a small skillet to pound the chicken to an even ½-inch thickness. If using cutlets, skip this step.

In a small bowl, stir together the Italian seasoning, salt, garlic powder, onion powder, and pepper. Sprinkle the mixture over the chicken and use your hands to ensure each piece is evenly seasoned.

In a large Dutch oven or pot, heat the olive oil over medium-high heat until it shimmers. Add the chicken in a single layer (working in batches if necessary) and cook until the first side is seared and golden brown, 3 to 4 minutes. Flip and repeat on the other side until the chicken has an internal temperature of 165°F. Transfer all the cooked chicken to a cutting board and slice into 1-inch-wide strips. Set aside.

MAKE THE PASTA: In the same pot you used to make the chicken, heat the sun-dried tomato oil over medium heat until it shimmers. Add the sun-dried tomatoes, onion, garlic, and Italian seasoning. Sauté, stirring constantly, until the onions soften, 2 to 3 minutes.

Add the broth and pasta and bring the mixture to a boil over high heat. Reduce the heat to medium-low so everything is at a low simmer, cover, and cook, stirring occasionally, until the pasta is al dente, 10 to 12 minutes. Remove the pot from the heat.

Stir in the arugula, parm, cream, artichokes, and sliced chicken. Return the pot to medium heat and cook for another 1 to 2 minutes, stirring occasionally, just long enough to warm the chicken and wilt the arugula. Serve with more parm for sprinkling.

Store leftovers in an airtight container in the refrigerator for up to 3 days.

Chicken Tikka Masala

Fun fact: Both of our husbands are originally from Pakistan. (No, they are not brothers.) So from time to time, we enjoy cooking up some of the recipes they loved to eat growing up. While our versions may not be entirely authentic, our husbands agree that they still very much get the job done. One of our favorites is this chicken tikka masala, where we douse chicken breasts in a yogurt marinade scented with paprika and garam masala before broiling them to juicy, charred perfection (our Minnesota version of a tandoor) and draping them in a creamy tomato-based sauce. Served over rice with plenty of naan for scooping, it's a meal the whole family gets excited to sit down to.

SERVES 4 TO 6

MARINATED CHICKEN

½ cup whole-milk plain yogurt

3 medium garlic cloves, minced

1-inch piece fresh ginger, peeled and grated

2 teaspoons garam masala

2 teaspoons sweet paprika

1 teaspoon ground cumin

½ teaspoon fine sea salt

½ teaspoon freshly ground black pepper

½ teaspoon cayenne pepper (optional)

1½ pounds boneless, skinless chicken breasts

TIKKA MASALA SAUCE

2 tablespoons ghee or extra-virgin olive oil

1 medium yellow onion, finely chopped

1 medium jalapeño pepper (optional), stemmed, seeded (or leave the seeds in if you want more heat), and minced

3 medium garlic cloves, minced

1 tablespoon grated fresh ginger

2 teaspoons garam masala

1 teaspoon ground cumin

1 teaspoon ground coriander

1 (15-ounce) can crushed tomatoes

¾ cup heavy cream

⅓ cup canned tomato sauce

1 tablespoon honey

FOR SERVING

Cooked basmati rice

Naan (optional), warmed

Finely chopped fresh cilantro leaves (optional)

MARINATE THE CHICKEN: In a large bowl, stir together the yogurt, garlic, ginger, garam masala, paprika, cumin, salt, black pepper, and cayenne (if using). Add the chicken and slather it well in the marinade. Cover the bowl with plastic wrap and refrigerate for at least 30 minutes or ideally overnight.

Preheat the broiler to high. Line a sheet pan with foil or parchment paper.

Arrange the chicken breasts in a single layer on the prepared sheet pan and broil until the first side is browned and slightly charred, 6 to 8 minutes. Flip and cook another 6 to 8 minutes. (It will continue cooking in the sauce.) Tent the chicken with foil and set aside while you make the sauce.

MAKE THE TIKKA MASALA SAUCE: In a large skillet, melt the ghee over medium-high heat. Add the onion and jalapeño (if using) and sauté, stirring occasionally, until the onion is soft, 5 to 7 minutes.

Add the garlic, ginger, garam masala, cumin, and coriander and cook, stirring frequently, for another 2 minutes, until the spices have released their fragrance. Stir in the crushed tomatoes, cream, tomato sauce, and honey and allow the mixture to come to a gentle simmer and continue cooking as you prep the chicken.

Cut the chicken into 1-inch cubes or slices and fold it into the sauce. Reduce the heat to low, cover, and cook until the chicken is completely cooked through and has absorbed the sauce, 6 to 8 minutes.

Serve over rice. If desired, serve with naan and/or garnished with cilantro.

Chicken Shawarma Two Ways

Chicken shawarma begins the way many Middle Eastern chicken dishes do: chicken slathered in a spiced yogurt mixture (which is truly our secret sauce when it comes to tenderizing the meat) and slow-roasted on a rotisserie. Luckily, though, you need only a couple of 16-inch metal skewers and an oven. The marinade does most of the heavy lifting when it comes to infusing this otherwise simple chicken dish with superior texture and flavor. You can then thinly shave and slather the chicken with all the classic fixings.

SERVES 8

CHICKEN SHAWARMA

1 cup whole-milk plain yogurt (Greek or regular)

3 tablespoons tomato paste

Juice of ½ lemon (about 2 tablespoons)

3 medium garlic cloves, finely grated

1 tablespoon extra-virgin olive oil

2 teaspoons smoked paprika

2 teaspoons ground cumin

2 teaspoons fine sea salt

1 teaspoon onion powder

1 teaspoon ground coriander

1 teaspoon freshly ground black pepper

8 boneless, skinless chicken thighs

SHAWARMA WRAPS

8 (8-inch) pitas

Sliced tomatoes

Sumac Onions (page 102)

Baba's Tahina Sauce (page 98)

Sliced Middle Eastern Pickled Cucumbers (optional; page 115)

Salatit Zabadi (optional; page 101)

Silky-Smooth Hummus (optional; page 94)

SHAWARMA BOWLS

Vermicelli and Rice (page 225)

Egyptian Tomato and Cucumber Salad (page 145)

Silky-Smooth Hummus (page 94) and/or Roasted-Tomato Baba G (page 92)

Sumac Onions (page 102)

MAKE THE CHICKEN SHAWARMA: In a large bowl, stir together the yogurt, tomato paste, lemon juice, garlic, olive oil, smoked paprika, cumin, salt, onion powder, coriander, and pepper. Add the chicken thighs and slather them with the seasoning mixture. Cover the bowl with plastic wrap and refrigerate for at least 30 minutes or up to overnight. (The longer they marinate, the more flavor they'll develop.)

When ready to cook, preheat the oven to 425°F. Line a deep baking dish with foil or parchment paper. You want to be able to lay the skewers across so the chicken doesn't touch the bottom, so choose a pan that works with the skewers you have. (This ensures that the chicken will cook evenly without steaming in its own juices.)

Divide the chicken between two metal skewers, firmly pressing the thighs together on each skewer. (This will help prevent the chicken from falling apart as it cooks.) Lay the skewers across the prepared baking dish and cover with foil.

Roast for 25 minutes. Remove the foil and roast until the juices run clear and an instant-read thermometer registers 165°F, another 25 to 30 minutes. Switch the oven to broil and broil until the meat is a gorgeous golden brown, 2 to 3 minutes.

Allow the chicken to rest for 10 minutes before shaving off slices with a sharp knife for serving.

IF MAKING A WRAP: Carefully slice the pitas into pockets and gently stuff with the shawarma and your desired condiments. Or, if using a larger Lebanese-style pita, you can pile everything right on top.

IF MAKING A BOWL: Layer the shawarma slices over the vermicelli and rice and top with your desired condiments.

Tips for Real Life

If you accidentally discard the vegetable juices, you can always use olive or vegetable oil to keep your hands from sticking when forming the patties.

Grill it: Preheat a grill to medium-high heat. Grill the patties until the first side has developed char marks, 7 to 10 minutes. Flip and repeat until the second side is charred and an instant-read thermometer inserted in the center of a patty registers 165°F, 7 to 10 minutes.

Grill-pan it: Heat a grill pan over medium-high heat. Lightly coat the grill pan with avocado oil (it has a high smoke point) and add the patties to the pan. Cook for 5 to 7 minutes until the first side is browned, flip, and cook for an additional 5 to 7 minutes, until browned and firm to the touch.

Air-fry it: Arrange the patties in an air fryer basket and air-fry at 380°F for 18 to 20 minutes.

These are also great as kofta kebabs. You could form the mixture around skewers and grill or bake for about the same amount of time.

Chicken Kofta Burgers

We like to think of chicken kofta as the original chicken burger. It maybe wasn't always served on a bun and stacked with tomatoes, Middle Eastern cucumbers, and a healthy drizzle of tahini (major oversight, in our opinion), but it has always been a way to transform ground chicken into pepper-stuffed, herb- and spice-infused patty heaven. So it's only right that we officially call for kofta to get the royal sandwich treatment it deserves. That said, you could also form this mixture into traditional oval kofta shapes and serve them with the standard condiments as we do with Mama's Beef Kofta (page 205).

SERVES 6

KOFTA BURGERS

2 small yellow onions, quartered

1 medium red bell pepper, sliced

1 medium jalapeño pepper (optional), stemmed, seeded (or leave the seeds in if you want more heat), and sliced

5 medium garlic cloves, peeled but whole

2 pounds ground chicken

2 teaspoons sweet paprika

2 teaspoons ground sumac

2 teaspoons fine sea salt

1 teaspoon ground cumin

1 teaspoon ground coriander

1 teaspoon freshly ground black pepper

⅓ cup finely chopped fresh flat-leaf parsley leaves

2 tablespoons tomato paste

¼ teaspoon baking powder

ASSEMBLY

6 brioche buns

Baba's Tahina Sauce (page 98), Yogurt Toum (page 111), or Spicy Zhoug Sauce (page 88)

Sliced Middle Eastern Pickled Cucumbers (optional; page 115)

Sliced tomatoes

Sliced onions

MAKE THE KOFTA BURGERS: In a food processor, combine the onions, bell pepper, jalapeño (if using), and garlic and pulse until roughly chopped. Transfer the mixture to a cheesecloth or fine-mesh sieve set over a bowl and squeeze or press out as much moisture as possible, reserving the liquid.

In a large bowl, combine the chicken, paprika, sumac, salt, cumin, coriander, and black pepper. Use your hands to thoroughly incorporate, then mix in the vegetable mixture, parsley, tomato paste, and baking powder until everything is evenly distributed. Cover the bowl with plastic wrap and refrigerate the mixture for at least 30 minutes or up to overnight. (We like to give it 3 to 4 hours for the flavors to meld.)

Form the mixture into 6 burger patties, about ⅓ cup each, dipping your hands in the reserved vegetable juice (see Tips) to prevent sticking and to impart more flavor.

Preheat the oven to 350°F. Line a sheet pan with foil or parchment.

Arrange the patties on the sheet pan and bake until the patties are golden and an instant-read thermometer inserted in the center of a patty registers 165°F, 20 to 25 minutes, flipping halfway through.

TO ASSEMBLE: Top each bun with a patty, your desired sauce, pickles (if using), tomatoes, and onions and serve.

One-Pan Turmeric Chicken & Rice

Chicken and rice is a staple of most busy cooks' playbooks, namely because it's inexpensive and you can likely make it with your eyes closed. Imagine how good it is when juicy chicken thighs get a golden makeover with an antioxidant-rich turmeric and smoky cumin marinade (no worries, it only takes 30 minutes), then are simmered in ginger-scented rice!

SERVES 6

TURMERIC CHICKEN

Juice of 1 lemon (about ¼ cup)

4 medium garlic cloves, minced

2 tablespoons grated yellow onion

1½-inch piece fresh ginger, peeled and grated (about 2 tablespoons)

1 tablespoon ground turmeric

1 tablespoon ground cumin

1 teaspoon fine sea salt, plus more to taste

½ teaspoon freshly ground black pepper

6 bone-in, skin-on chicken thighs

2 tablespoons neutral high-heat oil, such as avocado or vegetable

RICE

1 small yellow onion, diced

2 teaspoons ground turmeric

1 teaspoon minced garlic

½-inch piece fresh ginger, peeled and minced (about 1 teaspoon)

1 teaspoon ground cumin

1¾ cups low-sodium chicken broth

1¾ cups jasmine or basmati rice, thoroughly rinsed until the water runs clear

1 cup frozen peas

½ cup packed fresh cilantro leaves, finely chopped

FOR SERVING

Finely chopped fresh cilantro leaves

Sliced almonds, toasted (see Dry-Toasting, page 29)

MARINATE THE TURMERIC CHICKEN: In a small bowl, stir together the lemon juice, garlic, onion, ginger, turmeric, cumin, salt, and pepper. Rub the marinade all over the chicken, including beneath the skin. Place the chicken on a plate or in a baking dish, cover with plastic wrap, and refrigerate for at least 30 minutes or up to overnight. (The longer it marinates, the more flavorful it will get.)

When you're ready to cook, in a large skillet with the lid, heat the oil over medium-high heat until it shimmers. Add the chicken, skin-side down, in a single layer with room between the pieces. (You may need to cook it in batches.) Cook until the first side develops a deep brown sear, 3 to 4 minutes. Flip and cook until the other side is browned, another 2 to 3 minutes. Remove the chicken from the pan and set aside. (It will not be fully cooked at this point.)

MAKE THE RICE: In the same pan over medium heat, cook the onion, stirring occasionally, until translucent, 2 to 3 minutes. Stir in the turmeric, garlic, ginger, and cumin and cook, stirring constantly, until fragrant, about 1 minute. Add the broth and rice, stir to combine, then nestle the chicken back in the pan. (It's okay if it's a snug fit this time around.)

Bring the mixture to a boil, reduce the heat to low so it's at a simmer, cover, and cook until the rice is cooked and the chicken is tender, about 25 minutes.

Uncover and quickly stir in the frozen peas, cover again, and continue cooking for 5 minutes until the peas are bright green and tender and the rice is cooked through. Fold in the cilantro.

Serve sprinkled with more cilantro and the toasted almonds.

Store leftovers in an airtight container in the refrigerator for up to 4 days or in the freezer for up to 3 months. Reheat on the stovetop or in the microwave. You may want to add a splash of water or stock to help the rice fluff back up.

Tip for Real Life

This is another great dish for throwing in whatever vegetables you have on hand. Chopped bell peppers, zucchini, squash, carrots, potatoes would be great; add them with the broth and rice.

Tips for Real Life

For even more flavorful kofta, refrigerate the uncooked skewers for 1 hour or up to overnight before grilling them.

Bake it: Arrange the skewers on a sheet pan and bake in a 375°F oven for 20 to 25 minutes, flipping about halfway through, until golden and cooked through.

Mama's Beef Kofta

While our Chicken Kofta Burgers (page 201) are a modern reimagining of kofta, our beef kofta recipe pays homage to tradition. There wasn't a party, special occasion, or holiday where a platter of these weren't on the table, ready to bundle up in warm pita and dress with tahina, hummus, tomato and cucumber salad, and sumac onions. Then we'd eat the leftovers for days afterward, often crumbled over a bed of vermicelli and rice. No matter how many condiments you layered them with, the smoky, rich kofta were always the star. Our mom's secret was folding in soaked bulgur, which keeps the kofta from drying out. And we've since discovered that if you don't have access to a grill, you can also make this under a broiler. Either way you'll need 16 wood or metal skewers. If you plan to grill the kofta with wooden skewers, be sure to soak them in water for at least 20 minutes to prevent them from catching fire.

MAKES 16 KOFTA; SERVES 8

¼ cup fine bulgur wheat

1 large or 2 medium yellow onions, roughly chopped

3 pounds ground beef (80/20)

¾ cup loosely packed finely chopped fresh flat-leaf parsley

1 tablespoon baking powder

2 teaspoons fine sea salt

1½ teaspoons freshly ground black pepper

½ teaspoon ground cardamom

FOR SERVING (CHOOSE ONE OR SEVERAL)

Baba's Tahina Sauce (page 98)

Silky-Smooth Hummus (page 94)

Egyptian Tomato and Cucumber Salad (page 145)

Sumac Onions (page 102)

Pitas

Cooked long-grain rice

In a bowl, cover the bulgur with 3 inches of cold water. Soak for 1 hour, then drain well.

In a food processor, process the onions until pureed. Transfer to a cheesecloth or fine-mesh sieve set over a large bowl, squeezing or pressing out as much liquid as possible and reserving the liquid.

Working in batches in a food processor, combine the drained onions, bulgur, ground beef, parsley, baking powder, salt, pepper, and cardamom and pulse until it forms a cohesive mixture. You don't have to worry about overmixing; we were taught that more mixing results in more tender kofta.

Preheat a grill to medium-high heat (400°F).

Dip your fingers in the reserved onion juice, which will help keep the meat mixture from sticking to your hands as you form the kofta, as well as season the meat. (The OG kitchen hack!) Take a ⅓-cup scoop of the meat mixture and mold it around a skewer into a long sausage shape. Repeat with the remaining meat mixture, occasionally dipping your fingers back into the onion juice.

Place the skewers on the grill and cook, rotating them every 2 to 3 minutes, until they have deep grill marks on all sides, 8 to 10 minutes total. An instant-read thermometer inserted in the center should read 165°F.

TO SERVE: Serve with your favorite sauces and salads and plenty of pitas and/or rice.

Store leftovers in an airtight container in the refrigerator for up to 5 days or in the freezer for up to 3 months. Thaw in the refrigerator overnight and reheat in the oven or microwave.

Egyptian Fried Steak *(Buftek)*

The word *buftek* has its roots in the French word *biftek*, which translates to "beef steak"—and that's exactly what this dish is. A close relative of veal Milanese, this breaded and fried beef dish is one of Egypt's most beloved, and you will rarely find a dinner gathering that doesn't include this on the menu. But it's also perfect for a simple weeknight meal. Once the thin steak slices marinate in seven spice and onion juice (onion juice is the Middle Eastern secret to flavorful, tender meat!), they only need a quick dip in a paprika-seasoned dredge before frying up to a golden crisp. Serve this alongside Herbed Rice (page 222), Egyptian Baked Rice (page 226), or Egyptian Tomato and Cucumber Salad (page 145). Or for a true crowd-pleaser—and the way we serve it in our house on busy weeknights—with prepared store-bought frozen French fries.

SERVES 8

MARINATED STEAK

1¼ pounds thin-cut beef steak (about 6 slices), such as bottom round or top sirloin

1 large yellow onion, roughly chopped

½ teaspoon garlic powder

½ teaspoon sweet paprika

½ teaspoon seven spice, store-bought or homemade (page 28)

½ teaspoon fine sea salt

½ teaspoon freshly ground black pepper

TO FINISH

Vegetable oil, for deep-frying

1 cup all-purpose flour

1 teaspoon sweet paprika

1¼ teaspoons fine sea salt, plus more for sprinkling

1¼ teaspoons freshly ground black pepper

2 large eggs

¼ cup whole milk

1¾ cups plain dried bread crumbs

MARINATE THE STEAK: Line a clean work surface with parchment paper and lay the steak on top in a single layer. Cover the steak with another piece of parchment and use a meat mallet, rolling pin, or the bottom of a small skillet to pound the steak to an even ¼-inch thickness. (Alternatively, you could do this in a large plastic resealable bag.) Place the steak in a large bowl and set aside.

In a food processor, puree the onion. Transfer the puree and all the juices to a cheesecloth or a fine-mesh sieve and squeeze or press the juices over the steak. Discard the solids.

To the bowl with the steak, add the garlic powder, paprika, seven spice, salt, and pepper and rub into both sides. Cover the bowl with plastic wrap and let the steak marinate in the refrigerator for at least 1 hour or up to overnight.

TO FINISH: Set a wire rack on top of a sheet pan and set near the stove. Pour about 2 inches of oil into a large Dutch oven or pot and heat over medium-high heat. To test whether the oil is hot enough, toss in a pinch of bread crumbs. If they sizzle and rise to the surface in 10 seconds, the oil is ready.

Meanwhile, set up a dredging station in three shallow dishes: In one dish, stir together the flour, ½ teaspoon of the paprika, ½ teaspoon of the salt, and ½ teaspoon of the pepper. In another dish, whisk the eggs with the milk, ¼ teaspoon of the salt, and ¼ teaspoon of the pepper. In the third, stir together the bread crumbs, and the remaining ½ teaspoon paprika, ½ teaspoon salt, and ½ teaspoon pepper.

Line a clean work surface with paper towels and lay the steak on top. Cover with another layer of paper towels and pat the steak dry as much as possible. (This will help the dredge cling to the meat better, which means crispier steak.) Coat both sides of the steak in the flour mixture, shaking

MAKE IT AHEAD

Buftek can be prepped, breaded, and stored in a freezer-safe container in the freezer for up to 3 weeks. You can fry them directly from frozen; no need to thaw them first. Just increase your cook time by 2 minutes on each side.

Tip for Real Life

If you buy meat from a butcher, ask them to slice and pound the steaks for you—a huge time-saver.

off any excess, then dip in the egg mixture, allowing any excess to drip off. Finally, coat with the bread crumbs. Use your hands to really press the mixture onto both sides of the meat so it adheres well.

Work in batches so you don't crowd the pan (you can add more than 1 to the pan as long as it isn't overcrowded—if the steaks are too close together or the pan is too full, the steaks will steam instead of brown). Add the steak(s) and cook until the first side is golden brown, about 3 minutes. Flip and repeat, about another 3 minutes. (The steak is thin enough that it'll be cooked in this time.) Transfer the steak to the wire rack and immediately sprinkle with salt. Repeat with the remaining steaks and serve hot.

Store leftovers in an airtight container in the refrigerator for up to 3 days. To reheat, bake for about 10 minutes at 375°F or air-fry for 2 to 3 minutes at 350°F.

Steak Shawarma Bowls

Yes, there are two shawarma recipes in this book. And yes, you need them both. It just wouldn't be right to deny you the option of making one of our favorite quick dinners that brings together rich, succulent steak plus pepper and onions. The secret to unlocking the optimal flavor and texture of the meat is the marinade: a hit of acid from lemon juice and vinegar, plus many, many spices.

SERVES 4 TO 6

SHAWARMA SPICE BLEND

1 teaspoon sweet paprika

1 teaspoon garlic powder

1 teaspoon onion powder

1 teaspoon fine sea salt

½ teaspoon freshly ground black pepper

½ teaspoon smoked paprika

½ teaspoon ground cumin

½ teaspoon Aleppo pepper or red pepper flakes

½ teaspoon ground coriander

½ teaspoon ground ginger

⅛ teaspoon ground cinnamon

STEAK SHAWARMA

1½ pounds flank steak

Juice of 1 large lime (about 2 tablespoons)

1 tablespoon distilled white vinegar

2 teaspoons honey

3 tablespoons extra-virgin olive oil

1 small red bell pepper, sliced

1 small yellow bell pepper, sliced

1 small red onion, sliced

½ teaspoon fine sea salt

½ teaspoon freshly ground black pepper

FOR SERVING

Vermicelli and Rice (page 225)

Silky-Smooth Hummus (page 94)

Salatit Zabadi (page 101)

MAKE THE SHAWARMA SPICE BLEND: In a small bowl, stir together the sweet paprika, garlic powder, onion powder, salt, pepper, smoked paprika, cumin, Aleppo, coriander, ginger, and cinnamon.

MARINATE THE STEAK: Slice the steak against the grain into ¼-inch-thick strips. This will help keep the meat nice and tender. A trick for doing this is to lay the steak on a cutting board so that the lines in the meat (the muscle fibers) are running side to side (not up and down), and then slice across them.

In a medium bowl, whisk together the lime juice, vinegar, honey, and spice blend. Add the steak, making sure it's well coated with the marinade. Cover the bowl with plastic wrap and refrigerate for at least 30 minutes or up to overnight. (The longer it marinates, the more flavorful the steak will be.)

Allow the marinated steak to sit at room temperature for 30 minutes before cooking.

In a large skillet, heat 2 tablespoons of the olive oil over high heat until it shimmers. Add half of the steak, allowing any excess marinade to drip off first. Cook without stirring until the first side of the steak is browned and caramelized, 3 to 4 minutes. Flip each strip and cook until the second side is browned, another 3 to 4 minutes. Transfer the steak to a plate and repeat with the remaining steak.

Add the remaining 1 tablespoon oil to the pan, followed by the bell peppers, onion, salt, and black pepper. Cook, stirring, until the vegetables and onion are charred but still slightly firm, 2 to 3 minutes.

Return the cooked steak to the pan and cook for 1 more minute to meld the flavors.

Serve with vermicelli and rice, hummus, and salatit zabadi.

Middle Eastern–Style Beef Pot Roast

Braising a chuck roast until juicy and tender is a distinctly American preparation, and is especially beloved in the Midwest because of our long, cold winters when we want something cozy to tuck in to. We season the meat with a heady mix of cumin and coriander so the whole dish—from the falling-apart tender meat to the thyme-infused tomato gravy—gets a Middle Eastern makeover. We highly recommend that you go old-school and serve this over rice, mashed potatoes, or bread to soak up all that sauce, but then don't miss the opportunity to transform leftovers into pita sandwiches with Baba's Tahina Sauce (page 98) and Egyptian Tomato and Cucumber Salad (page 145). TBH, leftovers are one of the main reasons we make this to begin with!

SERVES 8 TO 10

1 chuck roast (4 to 5 pounds)

2 teaspoons ground coriander

1½ teaspoons ground cumin

1½ teaspoons fine sea salt

¾ teaspoon freshly ground black pepper

2 tablespoons all-purpose flour

3 cups low-sodium beef broth

2 tablespoons extra-virgin olive oil

1 pound carrots, halved crosswise

2 medium yellow onions, halved

1 tablespoon canola oil

¼ cup canned tomato sauce

6 medium garlic cloves, smashed

1 fresh thyme sprig

2 dried bay leaves

Mashed potatoes, cooked long-grain rice, or good crusty bread (optional), for serving

Preheat the oven to 275°F.

Pat dry the chuck roast with paper towels (don't skip this step, it will help the spice rub stick) and set aside.

In a small bowl, stir together the coriander, cumin, salt, and pepper. Sprinkle the mixture evenly over all sides of the meat and use your hands to make sure it's well coated. It might seem like a lot of seasoning, but trust us, it works.

In another small bowl, whisk together the flour and ¼ cup of the broth and set the slurry aside.

In a large Dutch oven or other ovenproof pot, heat the olive oil over high heat until it shimmers. Add the carrots and onions and sauté, stirring constantly, until they begin to brown, 2 to 3 minutes. Transfer them to a plate and set aside.

Add the canola oil to the pot, followed by the roast. Let it sear for 4 to 5 minutes (avoid moving the meat). After 4 to 5 minutes, take a peek. If it has a nice golden crust, go ahead and flip it. Sear the other side until deeply golden, 2 to 3 minutes.

Add the remaining 2¾ cups broth, the tomato sauce, flour slurry, cooked carrots and onions, garlic, thyme, and bay leaves. Cover the pot and carefully transfer it to the oven. Roast, ideally without opening the oven door, until the meat is falling-apart tender, 3½ to 4 hours.

Discard the thyme sprig and bay leaves, cover the roast with foil, and allow it to rest for 15 to 20 minutes before slicing and serving.

Spoon over mashed potatoes or rice, or sop up with bread, if desired.

Store leftovers in an airtight container in the refrigerator for up to 4 days.

Tips for Real Life

When buying a chuck roast, choose one that has plenty of marbling. Marbling equals fat, which equals flavor and tenderness.

It might seem like double work to have to cook the meat in the pan before transferring it to the oven, but giving it that seared crust is what locks in all the flavor and juiciness of the meat as it continues to cook in the oven.

If you check the meat for doneness and see that it's tough, don't panic! It's not overcooked. More likely, the meat isn't cooked *enough* and needs a little longer to loosen up and tenderize.

Make in a slow cooker: Add the seared beef, carrots, and onions to the slow cooker with the remaining ingredients and cook on high for 4 to 6 hours or low for 8 to 10 hours, until the meat is falling-apart tender.

Hummus with Spiced Ground Beef (*Hummus bil Lahme*)

The only thing better than a bowl of our silky-smooth hummus is a bowl of hummus heaped with warm, sultry seven-spiced beef. It's a dish you'll commonly find as part of a mezze or appetizer spread on our tables, at our family gatherings, and in restaurants, but there's no rule about enjoying it on its own as a light meal with all the pita or veggies you could possibly want.

SERVES 6

SPICED GROUND BEEF

1 teaspoon freshly ground black pepper

¾ teaspoon fine sea salt

½ teaspoon ground allspice

½ teaspoon ground cumin

½ teaspoon ground coriander

⅛ teaspoon ground cardamom

⅛ teaspoon ground cinnamon

⅛ teaspoon ground nutmeg

⅛ teaspoon ground cloves

1 tablespoon extra-virgin olive oil

1 small yellow onion, finely chopped

1 pound ground beef (85/15)

ASSEMBLY

Silky-Smooth Hummus (page 94)

Extra-virgin olive oil, for drizzling

Ground sumac

Fresh flat-leaf parsley leaves

Pine nuts or slivered almonds (optional), toasted (see Dry-Toasting, page 29)

Homemade Pita Chips (page 85), pita bread, flatbread, or raw or blanched veggies

MAKE THE SPICED GROUND BEEF: In a small bowl, stir together the pepper, salt, allspice, cumin, coriander, cardamom, cinnamon, nutmeg, and cloves. Set aside.

In a large skillet, heat the olive oil over medium-high heat until it shimmers. Add the onions and sauté, stirring occasionally, until translucent, about 2 minutes.

Add the beef, using your spoon to break it into fine crumbles as it cooks. Cook, stirring occasionally, until the beef is beginning to brown, 5 to 7 minutes. Sprinkle with the spice mix and fold it into the meat. Cook until the spices are aromatic and the beef is completely browned, 1 to 2 minutes. Remove the pan from the heat.

ASSEMBLE THE DISH: Spread the hummus over a plate or platter, creating a well in the center. Spoon the still-warm spiced ground beef into the well. Drizzle with olive oil, sprinkle with a pinch of sumac, and finish with parsley. If desired, add some toasted pine nuts or almonds into the mix too. Serve with pita chips, bread, or vegetables for dipping.

MAKE IT AHEAD

The hummus can be made up to 1 week in advance (or months, if you freeze it). The cooked beef mixture can be stored in the refrigerator for up to 4 days. Just reheat the beef on the stove before serving.

Tip for Real Life

If you have homemade seven spice (see page 28), you could use 2 teaspoons in place of the seasonings called for in the recipe (you still need to add salt and pepper unless your seven spice already has it included).

Egyptian Orzo *(Lesan el Asfour)*

In Arabic, the phrase *lesan el asfour* translates to "bird's tongue," a funny but not totally inaccurate comparison between the shape of orzo—a small, rice-shaped cut of pasta—and a bird's tongue. This dish combines ground beef and spices with the orzo for a filling and comforting sort of Egyptian Hamburger Helper, which is why our mom would often make it for us. Plus it's very simple to prepare and a budget-friendly way to feed a lot of people. It's a great recipe for reheating throughout the week, too—or making a double batch and stashing in the freezer for a rainy day.

SERVES 6

4 tablespoons extra-virgin olive oil

1 medium yellow onion, finely diced

½ cup finely diced red bell pepper (about ½ medium pepper)

6 medium garlic cloves, minced

1 pound ground beef (85/15)

5 tablespoons tomato paste

Fine sea salt and freshly ground black pepper

½ teaspoon ground cinnamon

1⅓ cups low-sodium beef broth or water

1 pound orzo

Finely chopped fresh flat-leaf parsley leaves, for serving

Bring a medium pot of water to a boil over medium-high heat.

Meanwhile, in a medium saucepan, heat 2 tablespoons of the olive oil over medium-high heat until it shimmers. Add the onion, bell pepper, and garlic and sauté, stirring constantly, until the onion becomes translucent, 2 to 3 minutes.

Add the beef, using your spoon to break it into fine crumbles as it cooks. Cook until all of the meat is browned, 5 to 6 minutes. Tilt the pan so the grease can accumulate on one side, then use a spoon or spatula to push the meat to the other. Very carefully use paper towels to soak up the excess grease.

Stir in the tomato paste, 1 teaspoon salt, 1 teaspoon black pepper, and the cinnamon so it evenly coats the meat, then cook until the tomato paste begins to caramelize, about 2 minutes. Pour in the broth, allow the mixture to come to a boil, then reduce to a simmer. Cover and cook until the liquid has reduced by about one-third, 4 to 5 minutes. Remove the pan from the heat.

While the beef simmers, add a generous pinch of salt to the now-boiling water. Add the orzo and cook according to the package directions.

Drain the orzo and fold into the beef mixture. Season with more salt and/or pepper, if needed, then drizzle everything with the remaining 2 tablespoons olive oil and give it one final stir. Serve sprinkled with parsley.

Store leftovers in an airtight container in the refrigerator for up to 4 days or in the freezer for up to 3 months. To reheat, thaw overnight in the fridge before warming on the stove. This slow thawing process helps maintain the dish's texture and flavor.

Egyptian Pita Sandwiches *(Hawawshi)*

This stuffed-pita sandwich is a handheld treat and one of the most popular street foods in Egypt. It's not much more than doughy pitas packed full of ground meat—typically beef or lamb, which you could use here instead—that's been given the full-flavor treatment from peppers, chiles, and warm spices, then brushed with oil and baked until cooked through, toasty, and oh-so juicy. But the real magic comes from loading these up with condiments like tahina sauce, pickles, tomato and cucumber salad, and sumac onions.

SERVES 4 TO 8

Extra-virgin olive oil, for the sheet pan

1 small yellow onion, roughly chopped

1 small red bell pepper, roughly chopped

1 small green bell pepper, roughly chopped

1 medium jalapeño pepper (optional), stemmed, seeded (or leave the seeds in if you want more heat), and roughly chopped

½ cup packed fresh flat-leaf parsley leaves

2 medium garlic cloves, peeled but whole

1 pound ground beef (80/20)

1½ tablespoons all-purpose flour

1 teaspoon sweet paprika

1 teaspoon fine sea salt

¾ teaspoon freshly ground black pepper

½ teaspoon ground cumin

¼ teaspoon ground coriander

⅛ teaspoon ground cinnamon

⅛ teaspoon ground cardamom

⅛ teaspoon ground nutmeg

⅛ teaspoon ground allspice

4 (8- or 4-inch) pitas

FOR SERVING (CHOOSE ONE, SOME, OR ALL!)

Baba's Tahina Sauce (page 98)

Sumac Onions (page 102)

Egyptian Tomato and Cucumber Salad (page 145)

Middle Eastern Pickled Cucumbers (page 115)

Preheat the oven to 400°F. Brush a sheet pan with olive oil.

In a food processor, combine the onion, bell peppers, jalapeño (if using), parsley, and garlic. Pulse until the mixture is finely chopped. Transfer the mixture to a cheesecloth or fine-mesh sieve and squeeze or press out all the liquid. (Discard the liquid.)

Transfer the drained onion mixture to a large bowl and add the beef, flour, paprika, salt, black pepper, cumin, coriander, cinnamon, cardamom, nutmeg, and allspice. Thoroughly mix until everything is well incorporated.

Wrap the pitas in a slightly damp kitchen towel and microwave for 15 seconds. This will steam the pitas and make them more pliable, which will make it easier to stuff them without tearing. (You could also do this in a 300°F oven for 2 to 3 minutes.) Use a small sharp knife to gently cut along the edge of each pita while rotating the bread with your other hand to create a slit along about half the length of the edge of the pita.

Stuff each pita pocket with ½ cup of the meat mixture. (Use the same amount for either size pita.) Use your fingers to gently encourage the filling down into the bottom of the pita and into an even layer. Arrange the stuffed pitas on the prepared sheet pan and brush the tops with a bit more olive oil.

Bake for 15 minutes. Flip the pockets and bake until the meat is browned and the pitas are crispy on both sides, another 5 to 10 minutes.

Serve with your favorite condiments and toppings.

Store leftover sandwiches in an airtight container in the refrigerator for up to 3 days. To reheat, bake at 350°F for 10 to 15 minutes, until crispy. Or air-fry for 5 to 6 minutes at 350°F.

Tips for Real Life

The size of your sandwiches will depend on how large your pitas are. If using larger pitas, you can halve each sandwich and serve up to 8 people.

Be sure to look for pitas that are thick enough for you to slice open and stuff.

Cheesy Stuffed Zucchini Boats

We told you that we Egyptians love a good stuffed-veg moment, and we would never miss the opportunity to pack tender, slightly sweet zucchini with a boldly flavored meat mixture flecked with olives (we also line the pan with meat to keep the zucchini juicy!). That said, we've brought a little bit of the Midwest to the table by draping everything in mozzarella cheese that gets nice and melty in the oven. We love that it's your meat and veggies all in one dish, in addition to the fact that it freezes really nicely if you decide to make a double batch. To make this vegetarian, see the Tips for Real Life below.

SERVES 6

1 tablespoon extra-virgin olive oil, plus more for the baking dish

1 pound ground beef (80/20)

1 small yellow onion, finely chopped

½ cup chopped green and red bell peppers (about ½ medium pepper each)

3 medium garlic cloves, minced

2 teaspoons Italian seasoning

1 teaspoon sweet paprika

1 teaspoon fine sea salt

¾ teaspoon freshly ground black pepper

¼ cup tomato paste

1 cup low-sodium vegetable or beef broth

⅓ cup pitted Kalamata olives

6 medium zucchini

1 cup shredded low-moisture mozzarella cheese

Tips for Real Life

Make sure you choose nice firm medium zucchini.. The bigger the zucchini, the more water they have, and the less firm they'll be as they cook.

Make it vegetarian: Swap out the ground beef for 2 cups cooked brown or green lentils (canned is fine), cooked quinoa, or your favorite meat substitute. Cook as directed above.

In a large saucepan, heat the olive oil over medium-high heat until it shimmers. Add the beef, breaking it apart with your spoon as it cooks into crumbles. Continue cooking, stirring occasionally, until the beef is no longer pink, 5 to 6 minutes.

Stir in the onion, bell peppers, garlic, Italian seasoning, paprika, salt, and black pepper and cook, stirring occasionally, until the vegetables start to soften, 2 to 3 minutes. Add the tomato paste, stir to combine, and cook, stirring, until it begins to caramelize, about 3 minutes.

Stir in the broth and allow the mixture to come to a boil. Reduce the heat to medium-low so it's at a simmer, cover, and cook until the liquid has slightly reduced, 3 to 4 minutes. Fold in the olives and remove the pot from the heat.

Preheat the oven to 350°F. Grease a 9 × 13-inch baking dish with olive oil.

Trim the stem ends of the zucchini and cut each in half lengthwise. Use a spoon to scoop out the flesh, leaving only a thin edge inside the skin to create "boats." Spread ¾ cup of the beef mixture over the bottom of the baking dish, which will help the zucchini cook and give it extra flavor. Arrange the zucchini boats on top in a single layer. Evenly divide the remaining beef mixture among the zucchini. If you have any remaining filling, add it to the bottom of the baking dish. Cover the baking dish with foil.

Bake for 20 minutes. Remove the foil and sprinkle the mozzarella over the zucchini. Continue baking, uncovered, until the cheese is bubbling and golden, about another 20 minutes. Serve right away.

Store leftovers in an airtight container in the refrigerator for up to 5 days or in the freezer for up to 3 months. Reheat in the microwave until warmed through.

Just Add Rice

Rice is a staple of Egyptian meals, and it was pretty much always on our dinner table—and honestly, still is. Rice was never an afterthought and it was *never* plain. So even though these dishes are technically side dishes, it didn't feel right to keep them out of the spotlight. Served with simply prepared vegetables and/or a protein, they easily become the stars themselves.

Herbed Rice *(Roz Mahshi)*

The same tomato-y, garlicky, spiced rice that usually shows up in stuffed vegetables in Egyptian cooking can also be a dish in its own right. It doesn't take any more effort or time than making a pot of plain basmati rice, and yet it makes even the simplest pairing feel like a complete and delicious meal.

SERVES 6

2 cups long-grain rice, such as jasmine or basmati, thoroughly rinsed until the water runs clear and drained

1 cup diced Roma tomatoes (about 2 medium)

1 cup packed mixed fresh herbs, such as dill, cilantro, and flat-leaf parsley (we use ⅓ cup each), finely chopped

½ cup canned tomato sauce

1 small yellow onion, diced

3 medium garlic cloves, minced

2 tablespoons extra-virgin olive oil

1½ teaspoons fine sea salt

½ teaspoon freshly ground black pepper

In a medium saucepan, stir together the rice, 1¼ cups water, the tomatoes, herbs, tomato sauce, onion, garlic, olive oil, salt, and pepper. Bring to a boil over high heat. Reduce the heat to medium-low, cover, and cook until the rice is tender, about 20 minutes. Uncover and gently fluff the rice with a fork and dig in.

Store leftovers in an airtight container in the refrigerator for up to 5 days. Reheat on the stovetop or in the microwave with a splash of water to help fluff the rice back up.

Tip for Real Life

You can stuff this full of veggies, if you want: Add ½ cup diced bell peppers (we like sweeter red, yellow, or orange for this) with all the other ingredients, and/or add 2 packed cups baby spinach after the rice is done cooking and heat it just long enough for it to wilt.

Vermicelli & Rice *(Ruz Ma Shareeyah)*

This blend of buttery Egyptian rice and toasted vermicelli noodles—or long, super-thin egg and durum wheat noodles—has a unique contrast of textures and a versatile flavor that adds interest to almost any savory dish. Use it as the base of a bowl, stir it into soups (especially Spiced Chickpea and Coconut Stew on page 157), or serve it next to your favorite veg or meat main.

SERVES 8

2 tablespoons unsalted butter

2 tablespoons extra-virgin olive oil

1½ cups vermicelli noodles

3 cups Egyptian rice (see Tip), thoroughly rinsed until the water runs clear and drained

4 cups low-sodium chicken broth or water

2 teaspoons fine sea salt

In a medium pot, heat the butter and olive oil over medium heat. Once the butter has melted, add the noodles and cook, stirring constantly to ensure even browning and prevent scorching, until they begin to turn golden, 3 to 5 minutes.

Add the rice and cook, stirring constantly, until the rice begins to turn opaque and smell slightly nutty, about 1 minute.

Stir in the broth and salt, increase the heat to high, and bring to a boil. Reduce the heat to low, cover, and cook until the rice is tender and has absorbed the water, 20 to 25 minutes.

Remove the pot from the heat and keep covered for 5 minutes.

Gently fluff the rice with a fork or rice paddle to separate the grains and make sure the noodles are evenly incorporated. Serve warm.

Store leftovers in an airtight container in the refrigerator for up to 1 week.

Tip for Real Life

Egyptian rice is a short- to medium-grain white rice that's traditionally paired with vermicelli. If you can't find it in your local Middle Eastern grocery store, feel free to use basmati or other long-grain varieties. You could also use sushi rice; you just have to be sure to rinse the rice very well to remove excess starch.

Egyptian Baked Rice *(Roz Maamar)*

This rice dish holds a special place in our hearts because we learned to make it from our father's mother, who learned the recipe from her own grandmother while growing up in her small Egyptian town. It's luxuriously decadent thanks to ashta, a thick, slightly sweet cream traditionally used in Middle Eastern cooking. (Though, you could also use clotted or heavy cream and get the same rich effect.) And while this is usually cooked low and slow in a clay pot, we've found that a Dutch oven or other heavy pot works just as well.

SERVES 8 TO 10

4 cups medium-grain rice, such as Calrose, thoroughly rinsed until the water runs clear and drained

1 tablespoon fine sea salt

1 tablespoon freshly ground black pepper

8 tablespoons (1 stick/4 ounces) unsalted butter, at room temperature

1 cup full-fat sour cream

2 cups low-sodium beef broth or milk

1 cup heavy cream or whole milk

1 cup ashta, clotted cream, or additional heavy cream or milk

Place an oven rack in the top third of the oven and preheat to 350°F.

In a medium bowl, stir together the rice, salt, and pepper.

Grease the bottom and sides of a large Dutch oven or other ovenproof pot with all of the butter. Do the same with the sour cream. Add the seasoned rice, broth, heavy cream, and ashta and *do not stir*. You can, however, give everything a gentle swirl without touching the bottom or sides of the pot. Keeping the bottom and sides undisturbed is what helps the baked rice develop its signature crust.

Cover and bake for 2 hours, until the rice is tender. Uncover the dish and switch the oven to broil. Broil until the top of the rice is golden, 2 to 3 minutes. Be sure to keep a close eye so it doesn't burn!

Remove the dish from the oven and allow the rice to sit, covered, for 30 minutes before serving. The steam will continue to soften the rice.

Serve immediately, being sure to add some of the browned rice to each serving.

MAKE IT AHEAD

If you want to make this earlier in the day, you can wrap the entire pot, including the lid, in a blanket or towel just after it comes out of the oven, which will keep the rice warm for up to 2 hours. The steam inside the pot will ensure that it stays nice and tender!

Cilantro-Lime Rice

This is not only a very simple way to dress up an otherwise plain bowl of white rice, but it's also a solid foundation for any number of meals—bowls, salads, tacos, burritos . . . even fried rice. We highly recommend keeping a batch in the refrigerator for the week; you'll be amazed at how often you find yourself reaching for it, especially if you're making Sumac-Spiced Whole Chicken and Onions (page 191), Spiced Chickpea and Coconut Stew (page 157), or Middle Eastern–Style Beef Pot Roast (page 210).

MAKES ABOUT 3 CUPS

1 cup long-grain rice, such as jasmine, thoroughly rinsed until the water runs clear and drained

2 teaspoons grated lime zest

1 teaspoon fine sea salt

½ teaspoon garlic powder

½ cup finely chopped fresh cilantro leaves

1 tablespoon fresh lime juice

In a medium pot, combine the rice, 2 cups water, the lime zest, salt, and garlic powder. Bring to a boil over high heat. Reduce the heat to low, cover, and simmer until the rice is tender and the water has been absorbed, 15 to 20 minutes.

While the rice is still warm, stir in the cilantro and lime juice until well combined. Serve warm.

Store the cooled rice in an airtight container in the refrigerator for up to 5 days.

Pretty Sweet

Dessert is our very favorite food group, and we have big opinions about what makes a good one. For as long as we can remember, as much as we enjoyed Egyptian and other Mediterranean and Middle Eastern dishes, we never really craved the desserts. Our mother's crispy, creamy kunefe? Yes. Baklava? One hundred percent. But oftentimes the traditional offerings were a little too syrupy and sweet for our Minnesota taste, especially after we discovered irresistible American classics like brownies, chocolate chip cookies, and cupcakes. So to put together the ultimate collection of dessert recipes for you, we've combined the best of all worlds. Here you'll find some of our beloved traditional recipes, our go-to Midwesternized treats, and then a mash-up of the two. (Think tahini cookies 'n' cream ice cream and Turkish coffee tiramisu.) What they all have in common is that they're quick, easy, and impossible to make just once.

Phyllo Rolls with Pistachios & Ice Cream

We went back and forth at least a dozen times about whether we should include a recipe for traditional baklava. While this flaky, nutty, sticky sweet Mediterranean and Middle Eastern dessert is a total staple of our fondest dessert memories, we thought we could leave all the fussing with the layers and layers of phyllo dough to the experts and instead give you a wicked-easy inspired-by version that you can pull together in 10 minutes. It has the same flavor profile (sweet, buttery, rich) and texture (melt-in-your-mouth), except with the very important addition of ice cream (or whipped ricotta, if you happen to have extra from page 261 on hand). Remember to leave time for thawing the phyllo!

MAKES 12 ROLLS

ROLLS

1 (1-pound) box frozen phyllo dough (14 × 18 sheets), thawed at room temperature for 2 hours or in the refrigerator for 6 to 8 hours

2 sticks (8 ounces) unsalted butter, melted

SIMPLE SYRUP

1 cup sugar

2 teaspoons vanilla extract

2 teaspoons fresh lemon juice

Fine sea salt

FOR SERVING

Chopped pistachios

Vanilla ice cream, or your favorite flavor

MAKE THE ROLLS: Preheat the oven to 350°F.

Remove the phyllo from the paper bag but keep the phyllo rolled into a cylinder. Place it on a cutting board and slice crosswise into 12 equal segments. Place each cut-side down in the well of a 12-cup muffin tin and pour the melted butter over the top of each, distributing it as equally as possible.

Bake until golden, 25 to 28 minutes.

MEANWHILE, MAKE THE SIMPLE SYRUP: In a small saucepan, combine the sugar and ½ cup water. Place the pot over medium heat and allow the mixture to come to a boil, giving it a gentle swirl or two. Reduce the heat to medium-low and allow the mixture to simmer until the sugar has dissolved, swirling occasionally, about 2 minutes.

Remove the pan from the heat and add the vanilla, lemon juice, and salt to taste. Gently swirl and set aside to cool slightly.

TO SERVE: Arrange the phyllo rolls on a serving platter and drizzle each with about 1 tablespoon of the syrup. Sprinkle with the pistachios and serve warm with ice cream and drizzled with more syrup and pistachios, if desired.

Store the phyllo rolls in an airtight container at room temperature for up to 1 week. Save the syrup in an airtight container and drizzle over the phyllo before serving; it does not need to be rewarmed.

Turkish Coffee Tiramisu

Whenever our entire family gets together for meals, there's always a pot of Turkish coffee to enjoy with dessert. While this strong, rich after-dinner drink can be an acquired taste, we realized that it's actually just the thing to use in place of espresso for dipping the ladyfingers for tiramisu. Be sure to plan ahead for this dessert; it needs to chill for at least 4 hours to set and meld the flavors, and can be made up to 2 days in advance.

MAKES NINE 3-INCH SQUARES

TURKISH COFFEE

3 tablespoons ground Turkish coffee

1 teaspoon sugar

ZABAGLIONE

1 cup sugar

6 large egg yolks, at room temperature

2 teaspoons vanilla extract

TIRAMISU

8 ounces mascarpone cheese

⅓ cup crème fraîche

1¾ cups heavy cream

½ cup whole milk

2 teaspoons sugar

30 ladyfingers

Unsweetened cocoa powder, for dusting

Tips for Real Life

If you're unable to get Turkish coffee, you can substitute espresso or use instant coffee. In both cases, you can simply stir them together with 6 ounces hot water and call it a day.

Instead of making one large tiramisu, you could portion the ingredients into twelve 8-ounce glass cups or jars for personal tiramisu parfaits, breaking up the ladyfingers as needed to fit. This is a fun way to serve this dessert for parties.

MAKE THE TURKISH COFFEE: In a 2-cup Turkish coffee pot or medium saucepan, stir together the coffee grounds, sugar, and 1¼ cups water. Slowly bring the mixture to a boil over medium heat, 3 to 4 minutes. Dark foam will start forming on the surface of the coffee as it gets closer to boiling (and that's okay!). Just as the coffee comes to a boil, add ¼ cup water. Bring the mixture to a boil once more and continue boiling for about 15 seconds. Remove the pot from the heat and set aside.

MAKE THE ZABAGLIONE: Fill a small pot with about 1 inch of water and bring to a boil over medium heat. In a heatproof medium bowl that can sit on top of the pot without touching the water, whisk together the sugar and egg yolks. Reduce the water in the pot to a simmer and set the bowl on top. Whisk constantly until the mixture thickens and increases in volume, about 10 minutes.

Carefully remove the bowl from the heat and whisk in the vanilla. Continue whisking occasionally as the mixture—this is the zabaglione—cools until it's only slightly warm, about 15 minutes.

ASSEMBLE THE TIRAMISU: Whisk the mascarpone and crème fraîche into the zabaglione until well combined and set aside.

In a stand mixer fitted with the whisk (or in a large bowl with a hand mixer), whip the cream on low speed and gradually increase the speed to high until stiff peaks form, 3 to 4 minutes. Be careful not to overmix the cream or it can curdle. Use a spatula to gently fold the whipped cream into the zabaglione mixture and set aside.

In a shallow bowl, combine 1½ cups of the cooled Turkish coffee with the milk and sugar. Dip each ladyfinger in the coffee mixture just long enough to dampen it. Do not soak for longer or they will get soggy and fall apart!

Arrange a layer of ladyfingers in a 9-inch square or 2-quart baking dish. Spoon half of the zabaglione mixture over the ladyfingers. Top with another layer of ladyfingers, followed by the remaining half of the zabaglione. Cover the baking dish with plastic wrap and refrigerate for at least 4 hours or up to 2 days. Add cocoa powder to a sieve and dust the top of the tiramisu before cutting into 9 squares to serve.

No-Churn Salted Tahini Cookies 'n' Cream Ice Cream

One of our first "real" summer jobs was at Dairy Queen, where we'd devour cups of Oreo ice cream. (I guess it shouldn't come as a surprise that we love a job with snacking perks!) It remains our favorite flavor, but we wanted to pack in even more of the good stuff, or what we like to think of as a Mediterranean Ben & Jerry's makeover. We added a creamy ribbon of tahini dulce de leche plus a swirl of chocolate/peanut butter ganache, but the best part is that you don't need an ice cream machine—instead everything is made in a mixer and gets frozen overnight.

MAKES 4¼ CUPS

CHOCOLATE SWIRL

¼ cup heavy cream

½ cup semisweet chocolate chips

ICE CREAM BASE

2¼ cups heavy cream

1 (14-ounce) can dulce de leche

⅓ cup well-stirred tahini

1 teaspoon vanilla extract

1 teaspoon flaky sea salt

10 Oreo cookies, roughly chopped

4 tablespoons creamy peanut butter
(we like Skippy Natural with Honey)

MAKE THE CHOCOLATE SWIRL: In a microwave-safe medium bowl, microwave the heavy cream for 1 minute. Add the chocolate chips and let them stand for 2 minutes. Gently whisk the mixture until it's smooth and resembles a thick chocolate sauce. Set aside.

MAKE THE ICE CREAM BASE: Line a 9 × 5-inch loaf pan with plastic wrap, leaving about 2 inches of overhang on each side. Set aside.

In a stand mixer fitted with the whisk, combine the heavy cream, dulce de leche, tahini, vanilla, and ½ teaspoon of the flaky salt. Mix on low speed until the mixture is well combined, about 1 minute. Gradually increase the speed to high and whip until soft peaks form, 2 to 4 minutes. Use a spatula to gently fold in the cookies.

Add half of the ice cream mixture to the pan. Dollop half of the chocolate swirl mixture and 2 tablespoons of the peanut butter evenly over the top. Use a knife to gently swirl the chocolate and peanut butter into the ice cream.

Add the remaining ice cream mixture to the pan and dot with the remaining chocolate sauce and 2 tablespoons peanut butter. Swirl once again and sprinkle the top with the remaining ½ teaspoon flaky salt. Fold the excess plastic wrap over the ice cream and freeze overnight.

Before serving, let the ice cream stand at room temperature for 15 minutes to soften slightly.

Store leftovers in a freezer-safe container for up to 3 months.

Our Favorite Chocolate Chip Cookies

The very first thing we ever made together in the kitchen was chocolate chip cookies. We followed the recipe on the back of a bag of Nestlé chocolate chips, and our mom agreed to let us do everything on our own (including cleaning up the kitchen). Even all these years later, we still love sharing a fresh batch of cookies—and gushing over how delicious they are (sometimes you have to be your own biggest fan!). After all this time, we've only made a couple slight tweaks to our go-to recipe—such as using brown butter and then chilling the dough before baking to give the cookies even richer, caramel-y flavor—and it's the perfect go-to recipe for chewy, cakey, gooey cookies. Just remember to double or triple the batch when you make these so you can freeze the portioned cookies for baking off whenever you need a fresh-from-the-oven treat.

MAKES ABOUT 16 COOKIES

10 tablespoons (1¼ sticks/5 ounces) cold, unsalted butter, cubed, plus 8 tablespoons (1 stick/4 ounces), at room temperature

2¼ cups all-purpose flour

¾ teaspoon baking soda

¾ teaspoon fine sea salt

¾ cup packed light brown sugar

¾ cup granulated sugar

1 large egg, at room temperature

1 large egg yolk, at room temperature

2 teaspoons vanilla extract

8 ounces semisweet chocolate (55% to 60% cacao; Ghirardelli baking bars are our favorite), roughly chopped

In a medium saucepan or skillet, melt the cold cubed butter over medium heat. Begin whisking or stirring with a spatula as the butter begins to foam (a good thing!). Continue whisking or stirring (which will help ensure the butter heats through evenly and prevent you from taking your eyes off the pan and cause the butter to burn) until the milk solids turn golden brown and the butter smells nutty, 5 to 7 minutes.

Remove the pan from the heat and immediately transfer the butter to a heatproof medium bowl. Continue to whisk or swirl the butter for about 3 more minutes in the bowl, which will help the butter cool, which will prevent it from burning. Set aside to cool to room temperature.

In another medium bowl, sift together the flour, baking soda, and salt. Set aside.

In a stand mixer fitted with the paddle (or in a large bowl with a hand mixer), combine the cooled brown butter, the remaining 8 tablespoons softened butter, the brown sugar, and granulated sugar. Beat on low speed to combine, then increase to medium-high and beat until just combined, about 1 minute. Pause the mixer and use a spatula to scrape down the sides of the bowl, then beat again on medium-high until the mixture is light and fluffy, 1 to 2 minutes.

Add the whole egg and mix until fully incorporated, 1 to 2 minutes. Stop the mixer and scrape down the sides of the bowl. Add the egg yolk and vanilla and beat once again to fully incorporate, 1 to 2 minutes.

Reduce the speed to the lowest setting. Add the dry ingredients and mix until just combined. You don't want to overmix or it will make the cookies too dense. Fold in most of the chocolate chunks, reserving a handful.

recipe continues >

Our Favorite Chocolate Chip Cookies (continued)

Tips for Real Life

We love making a double or even triple batch of these. You can store the unbaked cookies in a freezer-safe bag or container in the freezer for up to 4 months. Bake as instructed above.

It can be helpful to use a light-colored pan when browning the butter, which will help you see when the milk solids are getting darker.

When chopping the chocolate, be sure to create larger and smaller pieces, which gives the cookies a variety of textures. You could also use chocolate chips in a pinch.

Don't be tempted to bake the cookies until they're completely set in the center because they'll be too dry (and hard). Remove them from the oven when slightly underdone, because they'll continue to bake from the residual heat after they come out of the oven.

Portion the dough into ⅓-cup scoops and roll them into oblong balls that are taller than they are wide. (This helps them keep their thickness as they bake.) Arrange the dough balls on a parchment-lined nonstick sheet pan and press the remaining chocolate chunks into the top of each dough ball. Refrigerate overnight. (If you're in a hurry, freeze the dough for 1 hour before baking.)

Place an oven rack in the center of the oven and preheat to 350°F. Line two sheet pans with parchment paper or silicone baking mats.

Divide the unbaked cookies between the prepared pans with 2 to 3 inches between them. Keeping one sheet pan in the refrigerator, bake the first batch on the middle oven rack until the edges are golden brown and the centers are still soft, 11 to 12 minutes.

Remove from the oven and allow the cookies to cool on the sheet pan for 2 to 3 minutes before transferring them to a wire rack to cool completely. Repeat with the second batch.

Store the cookies in an airtight container at room temperature for up to 3 days.

Salted Sticky Toffee Pudding Cupcakes

We'd like to think the name says it all for these flawlessly moist, caramelly mini cakes draped in toffee sauce, but they're actually hiding one very surprising (and traditional) ingredient: dates. Dates add a delightfully sticky, jammy, and perfectly sweet but-not-too-sweet bite, which also happens to have a naturally caramel-like flavor.

MAKES 12 CUPCAKES

DATE PASTE

9 to 12 pitted Medjool dates (about 1½ cups; make sure they're soft and sticky)

1 teaspoon baking soda

CUPCAKES

Softened butter and flour, for the muffin tin

1¾ cups all-purpose flour

2 teaspoons baking powder

¼ teaspoon fine sea salt

8 tablespoons (1 stick/4 ounces) unsalted butter, at room temperature

1 cup packed dark brown sugar

3 large eggs, at room temperature

2 teaspoons vanilla extract

◖ SALTED TOFFEE SAUCE

¾ cup heavy cream

¾ cup packed dark brown sugar

8 tablespoons (1 stick/4 ounces) unsalted butter

1 teaspoon fine sea salt

FOR SERVING

Vanilla ice cream

Flaky sea salt, for sprinkling

MAKE THE DATE PASTE: In a medium saucepan, combine the dates and 1¼ cups water. Cook, stirring occasionally, over medium heat until the dates are soft and have absorbed the water, about 5 minutes.

Use a potato or meat masher or a fork to gently mash the dates until they're a smooth paste. Remove the pot from the heat and stir in the baking soda. The mixture will bubble up (and that's okay!). Spread the paste over a large plate and set aside to cool completely while you make the cupcakes. (The date paste can be refrigerated in an airtight container for up to 3 days and will need to sit at room temperature for at least 30 minutes before using.)

MAKE THE CUPCAKES: Position an oven rack in the lower third of the oven and preheat the oven to 350°F. Grease 12 cups of a muffin tin with butter and lightly dust with flour.

In a medium bowl, whisk together the flour, baking powder, and fine sea salt. Set aside.

In a stand mixer fitted with the paddle (or in a large bowl with a hand mixer), beat together the butter and brown sugar on medium-high speed until light and fluffy, 2 to 3 minutes. Reduce the speed to low and add the eggs one at a time, beating well after each addition. Increase the speed to medium-high, add the vanilla, and mix to incorporate.

With the mixer on the lowest speed, gradually add the flour mixture and mix until just combined. You don't want to overmix or the cupcakes will get too dense. Use a spatula to fold in the cooled date paste until it's evenly distributed throughout the batter. Divide the batter evenly among the muffin cups, filling each about three-quarters full.

Bake until the sides start to pull away from the pan and a toothpick inserted into the center comes out with just a few crumbs clinging to it, 20 to 25 minutes.

MEANWHILE, MAKE THE SALTED TOFFEE SAUCE: In a medium saucepan, combine the cream, brown sugar, butter, and fine sea salt. Set over medium heat and use a whisk or heatproof spatula to stir the mixture constantly

recipe continues >

Salted Sticky Toffee Pudding Cupcakes (continued)

Tips for Real Life

You want to buy soft, jammy Medjool dates. We like Sun Gold from Costco or Good and Gather from Target.

Make jumbo cupcakes: Prepare a jumbo muffin tin as described above and divide the batter evenly among the wells. Bake for 25 to 30 minutes and drizzle with about ⅓ cup of the sauce each.

Make a cake: Butter and flour a 10-inch Bundt pan or 9 × 13-inch cake pan and bake for 40 to 50 minutes. Drizzle with the sauce and serve.

If you would like to line your cupcake wells, be sure to use silicone liners; the cupcakes are too sticky for paper liners.

until it is completely uniform and smooth, 3 to 4 minutes. Reduce the heat to medium-low and continue stirring for 1 more minute to ensure that the sauce won't separate when poured over the cupcakes. Remove the saucepan from the heat and cover to keep hot. (You may need to gently reheat the sauce when the cake is out of the oven; you want it hot so that the consistency is nice and drizzly.)

While the cupcakes are still warm, invert them onto a deep serving platter, then poke them all over, all the way through, with a toothpick or wooden skewer—6 to 8 pokes each. Pour 3 to 4 tablespoons of the sauce evenly over each cupcake.

Serve topped with vanilla ice cream and sprinkled with flaky sea salt.

Store the cupcakes in an airtight container in the refrigerator for up to 5 days. If you want to warm them before eating or serving, pop them into a 300°F oven for 20 minutes or the microwave for 1 minute, or until warmed through.

Mama's Kunafa

Of all the Middle Eastern desserts that our mom would make for us, this was hands-down the favorite. It has a warm, custard-like center with a syrup-soaked shredded phyllo outside that melts in your mouth. Initially, we tried to simplify Mom's recipe, but then we asked ourselves, *Why?* The original deserves to be celebrated as is. And when the kunafa expert herself tasted our version, she did a double take because she couldn't believe we had managed to get that perfectly crisp outside and lusciously creamy inside. It's safe to say that we nailed it!

MAKES ONE 14-INCH KUNAFA
(SERVES 8 TO 10)

SIMPLE SYRUP

2 cups granulated sugar

1 teaspoon fresh lime juice

CUSTARD FILLING

2 cups heavy cream

1 cup whole milk

2 tablespoons all-purpose flour

2 tablespoons cornstarch

2 tablespoons granulated sugar

ASSEMBLY

1 (1-pound) package frozen shredded phyllo dough (also called kataifi), thawed

¼ cup powdered sugar

1 cup ghee, melted, plus more for greasing the skillet

MAKE THE SIMPLE SYRUP: In a medium saucepan, combine the granulated sugar, lime juice, and 1½ cups water. Set over high heat and allow the mixture to come to a boil, avoiding stirring to prevent the syrup from crystallizing. However, if the sugar is not dissolving, you can give it a few stirs. Once the mixture boils, stop stirring and allow the mixture to boil vigorously for 1 to 2 minutes. Reduce the heat to medium-low and let the syrup gently simmer for 10 minutes. Set a timer! You want the syrup to have thickened slightly, and be similar in consistency (but not color!) to maple syrup.

Remove the pan from the heat and transfer the syrup to a spouted liquid measuring cup or gravy boat. Allow it to cool to room temperature while you prepare the kunafa.

MAKE THE CUSTARD FILLING: In a medium saucepan, whisk together the cream, milk, flour, cornstarch, and granulated sugar until completely smooth. Set over medium-high heat and continue to slowly whisk the mixture until bubbles form along the edges and the mixture thickens, 5 to 6 minutes.

Transfer the mixture to a medium bowl and cover with plastic wrap, ensuring that the wrap is touching the surface of the custard to prevent a skin from forming. Set aside.

ASSEMBLE THE KUNAFA: Preheat the oven to 400°F. Grease an oven-safe 14-inch skillet with ghee and set aside.

Place half of the shredded phyllo in a food processor. Pulse until it becomes finely shredded, then transfer it to a large bowl. Repeat with the remaining phyllo. If needed, you can do this in more than two batches.

Add the powdered sugar to the phyllo mixture and stir until the sugar is fully incorporated and no longer visible. Drizzle ¾ cup of the ghee over the phyllo mixture and use your hands to mix until the phyllo is thoroughly coated.

recipe continues >

Spread a little more than half of the phyllo mixture over the prepared skillet, pressing it firmly into the bottom. Pour the custard over the phyllo, leaving a ½-inch border around the edge of the skillet. Loosely top the custard with the remaining phyllo, gently patting it down to cover all of the custard. Drizzle the remaining ¼ cup ghee evenly over the top.

Bake until the kunafa is golden brown, about 30 minutes.

When it comes out of the oven, immediately drizzle with the syrup. Serve straight from the oven, taking care to slice the kunafa gently or the custard will ooze out the sides.

Store leftovers in an airtight container in the refrigerator for up to 4 days. Reheat in a 350°F oven for about 20 minutes, or until warmed through.

Croissant Bread Pudding with Caramel Sauce

For a long time, the only bread pudding we knew was om ali, an Egyptian dessert made from crispy phyllo dough that is soaked in sweetened cream. Texturally, it was always a little too loose for our taste, but we did love the idea of all that buttery, flaky goodness holding things together. So we got creative and did things our way. The result? Bread pudding using store-bought croissants. They soak up the custardy base and create a rich, luxurious-feeling dessert that comes together effortlessly and can be made ahead.

SERVES 6

BREAD PUDDING

6 large croissants (preferably stale/day-old), cut into 1-inch-thick slices and left to dry out overnight

1½ cups whole milk

3 large egg yolks

2 teaspoons vanilla extract

CARAMEL SAUCE

1¼ cups packed light brown sugar

1 cup heavy cream

1½ sticks (6 ounces) unsalted butter

1 teaspoon vanilla extract

½ teaspoon fine sea salt

FOR SERVING

¾ cup sliced almonds, toasted (see Dry-Toasting, page 29)

MAKE THE BREAD PUDDING: Preheat the oven to 350°F.

In a 9 × 13-inch baking dish, arrange the croissant slices cut-side up in a double layer.

In a medium bowl, whisk together the milk, egg yolks, and vanilla until there are no white streaks. Pour the mixture over the croissants and set aside to soak while you make the caramel sauce.

MAKE THE CARAMEL SAUCE: In a small saucepan, stir together the brown sugar, cream, butter, vanilla, and salt. Bring the mixture to a boil over medium-low heat, stirring occasionally. Allow the mixture to continue boiling until the sauce thickens, about 3 minutes.

Pour half of the caramel sauce over the croissants and reserve the remaining half for serving.

Bake the bread pudding until the top is golden brown, 20 to 25 minutes.

Serve warm with the remaining caramel sauce and sprinkled with the almonds.

MAKE IT AHEAD

The caramel sauce can be made up to 4 days in advance and stored in an airtight container in the refrigerator once it's cooled completely. Gently reheat it in the microwave or on the stove until just warm. Simply assemble the dish just before it's ready to bake.

Tips for Real Life

If you need to buy fresh croissants for this recipe, you can slice the croissants and then leave them on the counter uncovered overnight to dry them out. Or if you're pressed for time, pop them into a 200°F oven for 20 minutes and then let them cool completely before using.

Use the leftover egg whites from this dish to make egg white omelets.

Pound Cake Berry Trifle with Lemon Mascarpone Cream

The secret to this dessert's effortlessness—and superior deliciousness—is store-bought frozen pound cake. Layered with cloudlike whipped lemony mascarpone and an assortment of deeply sweet macerated berries, it tastes like you spent all afternoon making the whole thing from scratch. It takes 2 hours to set in the fridge, but that time is completely hands-off.

SERVES 8 TO 10

MACERATED BERRIES

1½ pounds strawberries, hulled and quartered

1 pint blueberries

6 ounces raspberries

6 ounces blackberries, halved

¼ cup sugar

2 teaspoons fresh lemon juice

TRIFLE

2 (8-ounce) containers mascarpone cheese

1 (14-ounce) can sweetened condensed milk

½ cup sour cream

1 tablespoon vanilla extract

1 teaspoon grated lemon zest

⅛ teaspoon fine sea salt

2 cups heavy cream

1 (1-pound) frozen pound cake, thawed and cut into slices 1 inch thick

MACERATE THE BERRIES: In a large bowl, combine the strawberries, blueberries, raspberries, and blackberries. Sprinkle with the sugar and lemon juice and gently stir to mix well. Allow the mixture to sit for at least 30 minutes or up to 1 hour, stirring gently two or three times.

MEANWHILE, MAKE THE MASCARPONE CREAM: In a stand mixer fitted with the whisk (or in a large bowl with a hand mixer), combine the mascarpone, sweetened condensed milk, sour cream, vanilla, lemon zest, and salt. Whip the mixture on medium-high speed until just blended, 1 to 2 minutes.

Add the cream and whip on low speed until the ingredients are well combined, 1 to 2 minutes. Increase the speed to medium-high and whip until the mixture is thick, fluffy, and forms soft peaks, 3 to 4 minutes. Cover the bowl with plastic wrap and refrigerate until you're ready to assemble the trifle, up to 24 hours. You may need to rewhip for 1 to 2 minutes.

Cut each slice of pound cake into ½-inch-wide strips and set aside. Spread one-quarter of the mascarpone cream over the bottom of a 9-inch trifle dish or large glass bowl. Add an even layer of cake pieces over the top, followed by one-quarter of the macerated berries. Repeat these layers three more times, ending with a layer of berries.

Cover the trifle with plastic wrap and refrigerate for at least 2 hours or up to overnight before serving. Refrigerate leftovers for up to 3 days. The longer it sits, the better it gets because the cake will continue to soak up all those flavors.

Cookies 'n' Cream Pots de Crème

This recipe checks a lot of boxes for us. It's chocolate. It involves Oreos. It's easy. The velvety, sinfully decadent mousse doesn't require tempering the eggs; you can just toss everything into the blender before letting it set for a couple hours. And you can portion it into individual servings, so you can have ready-to-eat sweet treats throughout the week or a quick and easy dessert for company, especially topped with fresh fruit to add a refreshing contrast. It's essentially pudding cups for grown-ups and we make zero apologies for that.

SERVES 8

OREO CRUST

10 Oreo sandwich cookies

2 tablespoons unsalted butter, melted

⅛ teaspoon fine sea salt

MOUSSE

1 (8-ounce) semisweet chocolate baking bar (55% to 60% cacao), roughly chopped

2 teaspoons vanilla extract

1 teaspoon instant espresso powder (optional, but highly recommended)

¼ teaspoon fine sea salt

1¼ cups whole milk

¾ cup heavy cream

4 large egg yolks, at room temperature

¼ cup sugar

Fresh raspberries (see Tips), for serving

MAKE THE OREO CRUST: In a food processor, pulse the cookies into fine crumbs. Add the melted butter and salt and mix until the crumbs are well coated. Add 2 tablespoons of the mixture to each of eight 6-ounce ramekins. Use the back of a spoon or bottom of a measuring cup to press the mixture firmly into the bottom. Refrigerate the ramekins while you prepare the mousse.

MAKE THE MOUSSE: In a blender, combine the chocolate, vanilla, espresso powder (if using), and salt and DON'T BLEND. Just wait a second . . .

In a medium saucepan, combine the milk, cream, egg yolks, and sugar. Set over medium heat and use a heatproof spatula to stir the mixture until it comes to a low boil (small bubbles around the edges) and thickens enough to coat the back of the spatula, 5 to 6 minutes. Be careful not to let the mixture boil or the eggs will scramble!

Immediately pour the mixture into the blender with the chocolate. Remove the steam vent plug from the blender lid and cover with a thick kitchen towel to prevent any splatter and hold the lid in place while allowing some steam to escape. Blend the mixture until it's completely smooth, pausing occasionally to scrape down the sides of the blender with a spatula.

Divide the mousse base among the ramekins, about 6 tablespoons per ramekin. Cover each ramekin with plastic wrap, gently pressing it to the surface of the mousse to prevent a skin from forming. Carefully transfer the ramekins back to the refrigerator and allow the mousse to set for at least 2 hours or up to 4 days.

Serve these straight from the refrigerator topped with raspberries.

Tips for Real Life

We love pairing chocolate with tart, punchy raspberries, but these would also be delicious with strawberries, blackberries, bananas, or orange segments.

You could finish these with a dollop of whipped cream and a sprinkle of chocolate shavings or a dusting of cocoa powder. Or for extra-extra-fancy, make these in mini shooter cups.

Mango & Cream Tres Leches Cake

Traditionally, tres leches is a vanilla cake soaked with three kinds of milk (evaporated, condensed, whole) and topped with a simple whipped cream frosting. We've added a tangy twist with a buttermilk cake and a sour cream frosting, plus a tropical punch from fresh mango.

MAKES ONE 10-INCH CAKE (SERVES 8 TO 10)

CAKE

Softened unsalted butter and flour, for the pan

1 cup all-purpose flour

½ teaspoon baking soda

½ teaspoon baking powder

½ teaspoon fine sea salt

¾ cup granulated sugar

3 large eggs, at room temperature

1 teaspoon vanilla extract

¼ cup vegetable oil

½ cup buttermilk, at room temperature

CREAM SOAK

1 cup half-and-half

1 cup sweetened condensed milk

1 teaspoon vanilla extract

WHIPPED SOUR CREAM TOPPING

2 cups heavy cream

½ cup sour cream

½ cup powdered sugar

½ teaspoon vanilla extract

FOR SERVING

1¼ cups chopped or sliced mango (¼-inch pieces from 1 large or 2 to 3 small mangoes)

MAKE THE CAKE: Preheat the oven to 350°F. Grease a 10-inch round cake pan with butter, line the bottom with parchment paper, and grease the parchment. Lightly flour the inside of the pan and tap out any excess.

In a medium bowl, whisk together the flour, baking soda, baking powder, and salt. Set aside.

In a stand mixer fitted with the paddle (or in a large bowl with a hand mixer), combine the granulated sugar, eggs, and vanilla and mix on medium speed until the mixture is pale yellow and fluffy, 3 to 4 minutes. Add the oil and mix to thoroughly combine, about 1 minute.

Sprinkle the flour mixture over the egg mixture and mix on medium until just combined, about 30 seconds. Add the buttermilk and mix again until just combined, about 30 seconds, taking care not to overmix or the cake will be dry and tough. Pour the batter into the prepared cake pan.

Bake until the top is golden brown and a toothpick inserted into the center comes out clean or with a few crumbs, 20 to 22 minutes. Allow the cake to cool completely in the pan, about 1 hour.

Meanwhile, clean the stand mixer bowl and place it and the whisk in the freezer for 15 to 20 minutes. This will help you get the fluffiest, lightest whipped topping possible. (The fat content of the cream is what traps the air and makes it fluffy; if that fat warms, it can't hold on to the air as well.)

MAKE THE CREAM SOAK: In a medium bowl, whisk together the half-and-half, sweetened condensed milk, and vanilla. Run a knife along the edges of the pan to loosen the cake. Invert the cake just to remove the parchment, then place the cake onto a clean flat surface such as a large plate. Use a wooden skewer to poke holes all over the cake (be sure they go all the way to the bottom), then slowly and evenly pour the soak over the top. Set aside while you prepare the whipped sour cream topping.

MAKE THE WHIPPED SOUR CREAM TOPPING: In the chilled stand mixer bowl fitted with the chilled whisk, combine the heavy cream, sour cream, powdered sugar, and vanilla. Whip on medium-high speed until stiff peaks form, 2 to 5 minutes.

Use a spatula to spread the whipped topping over the cake. Dot the top with mango and serve immediately.

No-Bake Cookie Butter Icebox Cake

Something sweet after a weeknight dinner is pretty much a must, and for us the gold standard of midweek dessert simplicity is a dessert that you can prep once and eat all week, just like the Egyptian custom of layering tea biscuits with whipped cream, icebox cake–style. We also wanted to celebrate another surprisingly popular ingredient in Egypt: Biscoff cookies. Because of the British occupation of Egypt in the 1800s, you'll find all kinds of European holdovers, including these buttery, malty biscuits. We swapped the whipped cream our mom used to make for a more cheesecake-y cream cheese filling and layered it all up in a loaf pan to make a cake you can slice as you please. And the best part is that this gets better as it sits, which means you can make it ahead for company or have a week's worth of dessert with minimal hands-on effort.

MAKES 1 LOAF (SERVES 8)

6 ounces cream cheese, at room temperature

½ cup powdered sugar

1½ cups heavy cream

½ cup sour cream

⅓ cup Biscoff cookie butter

2 teaspoons vanilla extract

⅛ teaspoon fine sea salt

40 Biscoff cookies, plus more for serving

MAKE IT AHEAD

The icebox cake can be made up to 3 days in advance. Tightly cover it with plastic wrap and refrigerate until ready to serve.

Line the bottom and all sides of an 8½ × 4½-inch loaf pan with plastic wrap, leaving about 6 inches of overhang on two sides.

In a stand mixer fitted with the whisk (or in a large bowl with a hand mixer), beat together the cream cheese and powdered sugar on medium speed until the mixture is light and creamy, about 1 minute. Add the heavy cream, sour cream, cookie butter, vanilla, and salt and beat on low speed until combined. Increase the speed to medium-high and beat the mixture until medium peaks form, 30 seconds to 1 minute.

Spread 1¼ cups of the whipped cream mixture across the bottom of the prepared pan. Arrange a single layer of cookies over the top, making sure to really pack them in there and minimize the gaps between the cookies. If necessary, break some of the cookies to fit them properly. Gently press the cookies into the cream.

Use a spatula to evenly spread another 1 cup of the whipped cream mixture over the cookies. Arrange another layer of cookies on top, pressing them gently into the cream. Repeat this once more, finishing with the layer of cookies. You may have a few leftover cookies.

Use the overhanging plastic wrap to cover the loaf and transfer the pan to the refrigerator. Chill for at least 8 hours or (preferably) overnight to set.

Unfold the plastic wrap from the top of the loaf and carefully invert the pan onto a serving plate. Remove and discard the plastic wrap.

Slice the loaf into eight 1-inch slices and serve garnished with crushed Biscoff cookies.

OPTION: Melt Biscoff spread in the microwave for 20 to 30 seconds, just until runny, and drizzle over inverted icebox cake.

Banoffee Pie Parfaits

There's a local restaurant here in Minneapolis where they serve a delicious old-school banana pudding layered with Nilla wafers. We love a throwback dessert moment, so here's our modern glow-up version: banoffee parfaits. Biscoff cookies were always in our pantry growing up, so we use them instead of Nilla wafers here. These individual cups have the same great layered-pudding appeal as banana pudding, but have a more toffee-ish taste thanks to the Biscoff and nut crumble and layers of dulce de leche (we couldn't resist!), resulting in a dessert reminiscent of a British banoffee pie.

MAKES 8 PARFAITS

BISCOFF CRUMBLE

½ sleeve Biscoff cookies (about 10 cookies)

½ cup almonds

½ cup walnuts

½ teaspoon fine sea salt

2 tablespoons unsalted butter, melted

MOUSSE

2 cups heavy cream

1 (14-ounce) can sweetened condensed milk

2 ounces cream cheese, at room temperature

2 teaspoons vanilla extract

PARFAITS

3 ripe medium bananas with no brown spots, sliced

1 (14-ounce) can dulce de leche

MAKE THE BISCOFF CRUMBLE: In a food processor, combine the cookies, almonds, walnuts, and salt and pulse until the mixture is uniform and chunky. Add the melted butter and pulse until well combined. Set aside.

MAKE THE MOUSSE: In a stand mixer fitted with the whisk (or in a large bowl with a hand mixer), beat together the heavy cream, condensed milk, cream cheese, and vanilla on low speed until well combined, 2 to 3 minutes. Gradually increase the speed to medium-high and continue beating until medium peaks form, 3 to 4 minutes.

ASSEMBLE THE PARFAITS: To the bottom of each of eight 8-ounce ramekins or jars, add ¼ cup of the crumble, followed by 5 to 6 slices of banana, and 1 tablespoon dulce de leche. Top with ¼ cup of the mousse, then repeat the layers of crumb mixture, banana, dulce, and mousse. Finish with a teaspoon of crumble on each.

Chill the cups in the refrigerator for 1 hour before serving.

MAKE IT AHEAD

These parfaits are most delicious within 1 hour of assembly because otherwise the bananas begin to brown. However, you can prepare them ahead of time by making the crumble and mousse and storing them in sealed containers in the refrigerator for up to 3 days. Then slice the bananas and assemble just before serving, giving yourself enough time for them to chill.

Whipped Ricotta with Honey & Pistachio Puffs

Our mom was the queen of kitchen hacks before kitchen hacks were even a thing. Instead of spending hours making fresh baklava, she'd simply whip together ricotta and honey and spread the mixture between layers of puff pastry to bake up into creamy-crispy squares that got a sprinkle of pistachios and another drizzle of honey. Using frozen puff pastry means not having to fuss with phyllo dough (which can be finicky), and the overall effect is surprisingly baklava-like but with a fraction of the effort required—not to mention even more layers of flavor than what can sometimes feel too one-note (sweet on sweet on sweet). It's the ideal recipe for entertaining, especially because you can make the whipped filling ahead of time and cut the bars into friendly bite-sized pieces.

MAKES EIGHTEEN 3-INCH SQUARES

1½ cups whole-milk ricotta cheese

¾ cup powdered sugar

4 ounces cream cheese, at room temperature

½ teaspoon vanilla extract

⅛ teaspoon fine sea salt

½ cup heavy cream

All-purpose flour, for dusting

2 sheets (1 pound) frozen puff pastry

Egg wash: 1 large egg beaten with 1 tablespoon water

¼ cup demerara or sanding sugar

Chopped salted roasted pistachios, for serving

⅓ cup honey, for serving

MAKE IT AHEAD

The ricotta topping can be stored in an airtight container in the refrigerator for up to 2 days. You can assemble the puffs up to 2 hours in advance and bake when ready to serve.

In a stand mixer fitted with the whisk (or in a large bowl with a hand mixer), combine the ricotta, powdered sugar, cream cheese, vanilla, and salt. Beat on medium speed until the mixture is uniform and creamy, 2 to 3 minutes.

While mixing, gradually add the cream. Increase the speed to medium-high and continue beating until the mixture is light and fluffy, 2 to 3 minutes. Chill the mixture in the refrigerator while you prepare the puff pastry.

Preheat the oven to 400°F. Line a sheet pan with parchment paper.

Lightly flour a clean work surface. Use a rolling pin to roll out the puff pastry into a 10½-inch square. Use a sharp knife to cut the puff pastry into nine 3½-inch squares.

Place the squares on the lined sheet pan and prick them all over with a fork, leaving a ½-inch border. Brush the egg wash over the squares and sprinkle the coarse sugar just on the edges, creating a ½-inch border.

Bake until the puff pastry is golden brown, about 15 minutes. Allow the pastry to cool for 30 minutes.

Spread 2 to 3 tablespoons of the ricotta mixture over each puff pastry square. Top with a sprinkling of pistachios and a drizzle of honey. Serve immediately.

Moroccan Chocolate Walnut Phyllo Roll *(M'hanncha)*

Chocolate isn't often in Egyptian desserts, so we started to wonder . . . why not? It made us think about m'hanncha, a Moroccan dessert that reminds us of baklava with coiled layers of flaky phyllo and nuts. The biggest difference is that it doesn't include a honey soak/syrup (something we're not so sad about) and it *does* include chocolate (bingo!). We swapped the traditional almonds for walnuts as a nod to baklava, but otherwise left everything else as is because it's perfection. We especially love serving this at parties because you can either let guests break off bits to enjoy or add a just-right dose of drama with ice cream or whipped cream mounded on top.

SERVES 6 TO 8

SIMPLE SYRUP

1 cup granulated sugar

1 teaspoon fresh lemon juice

PHYLLO ROLL

1½ cups walnuts

¼ cup powdered sugar, plus more to finish

4 tablespoons unsalted butter, at room temperature

1 teaspoon vanilla extract

¼ teaspoon ground cinnamon

¼ teaspoon fine sea salt

4 ounces semisweet or dark chocolate, finely chopped

12 sheets frozen phyllo dough, thawed in the refrigerator overnight or at room temperature for 2 hours

4 tablespoons unsalted butter, melted

MAKE IT AHEAD

You can make the roll the day before you'd like to serve it and keep it at room temperature. It will get more delicious as it sits because it will fully soak up all the syrup, making it soft and buttery in the center but sticky and crispy on the outside.

MAKE THE SIMPLE SYRUP: In a small saucepan, combine the granulated sugar, lemon juice, and ½ cup water. Bring to a boil over medium heat, stirring until the sugar has dissolved. Remove from the heat and set aside to cool while you assemble the roll.

MAKE THE PHYLLO ROLL: Preheat the oven to 350°F.

In a food processor, combine the walnuts, powdered sugar, softened butter, vanilla, cinnamon, and salt. Pulse until a chunky (not super-fine) paste begins to form. Add the chocolate and pulse again until the chocolate is evenly distributed but not finely ground.

On a clean work surface, lay 3 sheets of phyllo dough with a short side facing you, side by side and overlapping the edges by ¼ inch. Brush the sheets all over with some of the melted butter. Layer 3 more sheets of phyllo over the first and brush with butter. Repeat twice more for a total of 4 layers.

Spoon the walnut mixture along the bottom edge of the phyllo. Carefully but tightly roll the phyllo up and over the filling to create a log. Brush the log with melted butter. Gently spiral the log into a coil, tucking the end underneath.

Carefully transfer the roll to a sheet pan or large ovenproof skillet. Brush the top with the remaining melted butter.

Bake until the phyllo is lightly golden, 18 to 22 minutes.

Remove the pan from the oven and immediately pour the syrup over the top of the roll. Allow the roll to cool at room temperature completely before serving, about 1 hour, or up to overnight covered with foil (it gets better as it sits!). Dust with powdered sugar before serving.

Slice into 2-inch pieces and serve or let everyone break off their own pieces.

Store leftovers in an airtight container at room temperature for up to 4 days.

Triple-Chocolate Hazelnut Skillet Brownie

Nutella is another one of those surprising ingredients that's very popular in Egypt. In fact, we were first introduced to it when our cousins there showed us how to eat it by slathering it over French bread or just inhaling it by the spoonful (to date our favorite way to enjoy it). It doesn't really need much to make it any more delicious, but that doesn't mean we couldn't try . . . since we're huge chocolate lovers, we wanted to triple-down on all that hazelnutty-fudgy goodness and add Nutella, chocolate chunks, *and* chocolate chips to rich, gooey brownies. They get baked right in a skillet for an oven-to-table showstopping moment, especially when served warm topped with ice cream.

MAKES ONE 12-INCH BROWNIE (SERVES 8)

Softened unsalted butter, for the skillet

12 ounces semisweet chocolate chips (we like Ghirardelli or Guittard)

1½ sticks (6 ounces) unsalted butter

⅓ cup all-purpose flour

2 teaspoons instant espresso powder

1½ teaspoons baking powder

½ teaspoon fine sea salt

3 large eggs, at room temperature

½ cup sugar

⅓ cup Nutella or your favorite chocolate-hazelnut spread

2 teaspoons vanilla extract

4 ounces dark chocolate (60% cacao), roughly chopped

Vanilla ice cream (optional), for serving

MAKE IT AHEAD

You can prepare the batter up to 3 days in advance and store it covered in plastic wrap in the refrigerator until you're ready to bake. Allow it to come to room temperature for 30 minutes, then bake as directed.

Preheat the oven to 350°F. Grease an oven-safe 12-inch skillet with butter.

Add the chocolate chips to a large heatproof bowl. In a small pot, melt the 1½ sticks butter over medium heat. Once the butter is totally melted, pour it over the chocolate and let the mixture sit for 5 minutes. Then whisk until the chocolate is completely melted and smooth. Allow the mixture to cool to room temperature, about 10 minutes.

In a medium bowl, combine the flour, espresso powder, baking powder, and salt and mix well.

Add the eggs, sugar, Nutella, and vanilla to the cooled chocolate mixture and whisk until smooth. Add the flour mixture and use a spatula to gently fold it in until there are no more flour streaks. Avoid overmixing or your brownies can toughen up instead of staying nice and soft. Fold in the chopped dark chocolate just until the pieces are evenly distributed. Pour the batter into the prepared skillet.

Bake until the top is crisp and there is a slight jiggle when you shake the skillet, 25 to 32 minutes (25 if you prefer a gooey, pudding-like center and 30 to 32 minutes if you like a more set brownie).

Let the brownie cool in the pan for 10 minutes before serving.

Serve warm from the skillet and topped with ice cream, if desired.

Store leftovers in an airtight container in the refrigerator for up to 4 days. To reheat, bake at 350°F for 15 to 20 minutes, until warmed through.

Tips for Real Life

The espresso powder helps the chocolate flavor really pop, but you can leave it out, if you prefer.

Make traditional brownies: Line a 9 × 13-inch baking dish with parchment paper, leaving an inch or two of overhang on each end. Add the batter and bake at 350°F until set in the center, about 35 minutes. Allow the brownies to cool in the pan for 10 minutes before using the parchment handles to carefully transfer them to a cutting board. Slice and enjoy!

Egyptian Lemonade *(Limonana)*

We recently shared a version of this recipe on our platform, and it instantly became the drink of the summer. But even though it was a huge viral craze, to us it's anything but trendy; it's the taste of our childhood. Aunt Eman, our mom's sister, would make this traditional cooling drink for us whenever we'd visit Egypt in the summer, where it often reached over 100°F on just an average day. Her signature touch was adding milk, which made the lemonade extra creamy. And yes, we still call it lemonade even though it's made with limes because Egyptian lemons are sort of a hybrid of the two. The closest we can get here in the States to their perfectly balanced sweet-tartness is a key lime, so there you go.

MAKES 4 CUPS

5 key limes or 4 medium limes, rinsed and dried (halve the limes if you don't have a high-powered blender), plus more sliced for garnish

3 cups whole milk

1 cup sugar

6 fresh mint leaves, plus more for garnish

Ice cubes, for serving

In a high-powered blender, combine the limes (yes—rind, seeds, and all!), milk, 1 cup cold water, the sugar, and mint. Blend just until the limes are broken down, about 30 seconds—the mixture might still be not 100 percent smooth. Do not overmix or the drink will develop a bitter taste.

Pour the mixture through a fine-mesh sieve to remove any pulp or solids. Transfer the limonana to a pitcher and serve over ice, garnished with lime slices and mint leaves.

Tips for Real Life

To make this dairy-free you can use nondairy milk. Just be mindful that it may affect the flavor of the limonana. If you're a fan of coconut milk, give canned coconut milk a try! (Emphasis on *canned* because it's thicker and creamier than coconut milk from a carton.)

For the best taste and texture, enjoy this drink right after it's made. After about 30 minutes it will start to separate.

All Dolled Up

We can't remember a time when we didn't love a party. It's most likely because whenever our entire extended family would get together, the house would fill with twenty or so people talking over each other, laughing, and just generally excited to be in the same place at the same time, making any occasion feel like a celebration. Our mom started cooking the night before, then by the time everyone arrived, the dining room table would be buried under platters and platters of entirely too much food. And we'd have it no other way.

What this taught us was that with the right amount of planning, attention to the details that matter (i.e., the ones that make guests feel comfortable and relaxed and your space seem intentional and polished), and a thoughtful selection of dishes, you can make even the most everyday nonoccasion occasion really, really special—and without a ton of work!

Teatime Tray

Teatime is one of our favorite cold-weather traditions and a perfect mash-up of our MidEast/Midwest upbringing. In Minnesota, winters are all about staying cozy in front of a fire and sipping something warm, but in Egypt, teatime is a daily afternoon ritual, no matter the season. If someone should happen to come by for a visit, the proper thing to do is to pull out any desserts or other snacky items you have lying around and to present them nicely on a tray for your guest—with black tea, of course. But you can go with any tea you like, or a selection of different teas for your guests to choose from.

TEA

Black tea (1 tea bag or 1 tablespoon loose tea per person)

Assorted herbal or flavored teas (optional)

Whole milk (or milk of your choice) if serving black tea

Honey and/or sugar

Fresh mint leaves

SNACKING

Assorted whole seasonal fruit: We like grapes, figs, berries, and citrus

Assorted sliced seasonal fruit: citrus segments, strawberries, kiwi, stone fruit

Assorted roasted nuts: almonds, walnuts, pecans, cashews, pistachios

A quick bread or simple cake: such as Upside-Down Walnut and Honey Banana Bread (page 54), cut into 1-inch-thick slices

OPTIONAL

Bite-sized sweets: Portion our Pound Cake Berry Trifle (page 251), No-Bake Cookie Butter Icebox Cake (page 256), or Turkish Coffee Tiramisu (page 235) into small slices or assemble them in shooter cups.

Assorted pastries: mini fruit tarts, éclairs, cream puffs, Danish pastries, croissants.

Assorted cookies: chocolate chip, shortbread, biscotti, macarons, Linzer, thumbprint. Go for a variety of sizes, shapes, and colors.

Sprigs of fresh herbs and/or edible flowers, for garnish, optional

PREPARE THE TEA SERVICE: Add the tea bags or loose tea to a teapot. In a kettle, heat 2 cups water for every serving of tea to a boil over medium-high heat. Pour it over the tea and let steep for 5 minutes. Remove the tea bags or, if using loose tea, use a strainer when serving the tea. Set the teapot on a tea tray.

In a small pot, place about ¼ cup milk for every cup of tea you think you're going to serve (count on 1 to 2 cups per person). Over low heat, gently warm the milk until it's just hot to the touch. Remove the pot from the heat and transfer the milk to a second teapot to keep warm.

Add honey and/or sugar to individual small bowls and place on the tea tray.

SET UP THE SNACKS: Mound the whole fruit as a focal point in the center of a large flat-bottomed platter or decorative tray. Fan the sliced cakes around the fruit, alternating with small bowls of sliced fruit and nuts. If hosting a crowd, also alternate in any pastries or cookies you've decided to serve. Keep an eye out for balance; you want there to be a variety of height, size, and color, which is what makes people want to dive in. Label any items, including any potential allergens (dairy, gluten, nuts), so your guests know what's what. Garnish with the herbs and/or flowers, if desired.

On the tray with the teapots and honey and/or sugar, arrange some mint leaves in a small bowl. Be sure to include serving utensils for the items on both trays (small tongs, serving spoons), so guests can easily serve themselves.

Give each guest a small tea glass, saucer, teaspoon, dessert plate, and dessert fork. Pour tea into each glass—the customary job for the host!—and, if desired, add a mint leaf to steep, too. Enjoy the afternoon.

Brunch Mezze Charcuterie Board (menu follows)

Brunch Mezze Charcuterie Board

This is one of our favorite spreads for entertaining. The inspiration is mainly the fact that, for us, breakfast or brunch usually means a big savory feast, which is something fun and different for many of our friends. We like to pull out all the stops to assemble a collection of Mediterranean and Middle Eastern morning classics, served up mezze-style. Mezze basically is an assortment of small dishes meant to be grazed over for a light-ish meal. Think dips and spreads like hummus, baba ghanoush, and labneh; falafel and tabbouleh; and plenty of pickles, dried fruit, cheeses, and nuts; all served with an assortment of breads for swabbing, dunking, and wrapping up like an Egyptian breakfast burrito. But what makes this set-up even more fun is the fact that it's a chance to get everyone together in the early part of the day, meaning you can linger over tea or coffee while the kids can entertain themselves, leftovers can do double-duty as dinner, and all the dishes will be done and put away well before bedtime.

This is a great opportunity to make things ahead, as well as to take advantage of your local Middle Eastern grocery store, where you can find many of these items premade. You can also slice all the fruit and veggies ahead of time, as well as portion everything into bowls. Or if you really want to take a load off in the morning, you could assemble the entire tray the night before, cover it with plastic wrap, and stash it in the fridge until about 30 minutes before guests arrive, then warm the bread.

IF SERVING A LARGER CROWD (8 TO 12), WE'D MAKE EVERYTHING ON THIS LIST WITH 1 TO 2 PITAS OR FLATBREADS PER PERSON. (IT'S ENOUGH FOR THERE TO BE LEFTOVERS TO SEND HOME WITH GUESTS.) IF SERVING FEWER PEOPLE, WE'D GO WITH THE FALAFEL, FUL, TABBOULEH, PLUS TWO SIDES AND 1 TO 2 PITAS OR FLATBREADS PER PERSON.

Mama's Egyptian Falafel (page 40)

Egyptian Fava Bean Salad (page 58)

Quinoa Tabbouleh with Lime Vinaigrette (page 118)

Baked or air-fried Halloumi cheese (see Tips, page 74)

Halved hard-boiled eggs (see Tip, page 141)

Sliced cured meats: We love pastirma, a Turkish cured beef

Pickles: turnips, cucumbers, pepperoncini

Little bites: marinated feta cubes, marinated olives

Raw vegetables: sliced cucumber, sliced radishes, carrot sticks, cherry tomatoes

Salted roasted nuts: almonds, walnuts, pistachios, cashews

Fresh fruit: grapes, pomegranates, citrus

Dried fruit: dates, figs

Assorted flatbreads: pita, lavash, za'atar bread, warmed (see Warming Pitas, page 29) and cut into quarters

Transfer any spreads and other "juicy" items (such as olives, pickles, or fruit) to small or medium serving bowls. Arrange the bowls on a large platter or decorative tray. Between the bowls, create small groupings of all the other components, creating a variety of color and shape on the platter. Label any items, including any potential allergens (dairy, gluten, nuts), so your guests know what's what. Serve with small plates and forks or toothpicks for guests to help themselves.

The Entire Family's Coming for Dinner Buffet

This epic feast isn't reserved for family occasions, but it will certainly make any acquaintance lucky enough to score an invite feel like they just made it into your inner circle. That's partially because this slightly over-the-top assortment of traditional dishes is so incredibly delicious, but it's mainly owing to how comforting it is to be welcomed in, taken care of, and not allowed to leave until your belly is a *little* too full. This is the spread that says, "I care."

Yes, there are a lot of dishes here—and this is exactly what our table looks like when the family comes over—but feel free to pick and choose. The beauty of these dishes is that they can be seamlessly mixed and matched because their flavors all complement one another. Many of them could also be made ahead. And, if we're being honest, many of them can be purchased already prepared! We start with the spreads, dips, and mains and then clear the table and get ready to put out the sweets and drinks.

THE MENU (SERVES 6 TO 8)

FOR SPREADING AND DIPPING

Roasted-Tomato Baba G (page 92)

Silky-Smooth Hummus (page 94)

Herby Roasted Olives (page 104) with Whipped Feta (page 103)

Baba's Tahina Sauce (page 98)

Plenty of pita (we recommend 1 pita per person), warmed (see Warming Pita, page 29)

THE MAIN EVENT

Egyptian Tomato and Cucumber Salad (page 145)

Quinoa Tabbouleh with Lime Vinaigrette (page 118)

Chicken Shawarma (page 198)

Mama's Beef Kofta (page 205)

Egyptian Orzo (page 215)

Creamy Chicken Spaghetti Bake (page 192)

SWEETS

Mama's Kunafa (page 245)

Whipped Ricotta with Honey and Pistachio Puffs (page 261)

Turkish Coffee Tiramisu (page 235)

Moroccan Chocolate Walnut Phyllo Roll (page 262)

TO DRINK

Tea (page 271) and Turkish coffee (page 235)

Egyptian Lemonade (page 266)

Soda (or pop, as we say in Minnesota)

Set out plates, silverware, and napkins before your guests arrive. Then we like putting everything savory on the table at once so that everyone can help themselves and graze as the evening goes on. Label any items, including any potential allergens (dairy, gluten, nuts), so your guests know what's what. When there's a lull in the action, we clear the table and set out dessert and tea.

Dessert Bar Cart

We love entertaining and love a good "bar," a curated edible setup that looks as gorgeous and playful as it is tasty to dive into. A dessert bar cart is one of our go-to arrangements whenever we have people over or just want a fun little treat for our families—it's become one of our signatures that people are always asking us for more of. We like featuring a selection of homemade and store-bought items so there's something for everyone without needing to make a ton from scratch. Plus, it gives us a chance to put out all the treats we keep stocked in our pantries for whenever guests happen to be stopping by. (Offering sweet treats to visitors is a classic Egyptian hospitality touch.) Feel free to get creative with this setup; you could also use a cart to showcase a selection of savory snacks, teas, even a little mezze buffet!

SELECT A CART

Remember that whatever you choose can (and should!) also be a permanent feature in your kitchen, living room, or dining room as a functional piece of furniture, whether you stock it with your favorite spirits, coffee and tea, or nonfood or beverage items. So, choose one that complements your style and fits your space (we always lean toward a more modern/chic/glam look). If you buy one that's vintage, make sure it's nice and sturdy. And for an inexpensive yet clean and streamlined option, you could buy a tiered wheeled cart (which happens to make a great art cart for your kids when you're all done!). You could also just put out this spread on a table, and no one will judge you!

CURATE YOUR DESSERTS

Aim to have a variety of textures and flavors, as well as mini sizes of things so everyone can try multiple items. We like to plan for everyone to have at least two of everything. Great options are:

- Mini cupcakes
- Mini cakes or cake pops
- Brownies and/or blondies
- Cookies
- Macarons
- Fruit tartlets
- Cups of mousse or pudding
- Our Favorite Chocolate Chip Cookies (page 239)
- Cookies 'n' Cream Pots de Crème (page 252)

PICK SERVEWARE

Select an array of serving platters, cake stands, and trays that match your cart and vary in size and height. Arrange them on the cart. (You might have to play around with different configurations.)

ARRANGE THE DESSERTS

To help the spread look balanced, place larger items on lower plates and platters, and perch smaller items on taller cake stands.

LABEL EVERYTHING

Make a little placard for each dessert, including any potential allergens (dairy, gluten, nuts), so your guests know what's what.

EMBELLISH WITH DECORATIVE ELEMENTS

Add a splash more interest with fresh flowers, edible glitter, or decorations that fit your theme. Give some thought to coordinating the color palette of these components with your cart and the desserts.

OFFER BEVERAGES

Consider including a variety of drinks such as coffee, tea, sparkling water, and juices.

DON'T FORGET THE TAKE-HOME DESSERT BOXES!

Buy small cardboard to-go boxes so your guests can take home any leftovers with them. It makes cleanup a breeze!

Acknowledgments

Never in our wildest dreams did we think that we'd be writing the acknowledgments for our very own cookbook—let alone writing an entire cookbook! This process has been so incredibly rewarding, thanks in large part to the many people who contributed in their own unique and special ways:

Raquel Pelzel: From the start, you understood our vibe and gave us the freedom to be creative; you had confidence in us. Your presence has been a breath of fresh air throughout this journey. Whenever we found ourselves in panic mode, you were there to guide us with patience. Thank you for standing by our side and navigating us through every step of this process!

Janis Donnaud: We are beyond grateful that our paths crossed! You're an absolute powerhouse. From our very first encounter, we knew you were the perfect fit for us. Your unwavering support and commitment to letting us be ourselves has meant the world to us. Thank you for believing in us!

Rachel Holtzman: Where do we even begin? Your contribution has been invaluable. You've not only helped us articulate our thoughts, but also ensured that our authenticity shines through every word. Your guidance, expertise, and support have been instrumental throughout this journey. You inspire us daily, and we couldn't have asked for a better copilot. Thank you for believing in us; we are forever grateful.

Marysarah Quinn: Your warmth and kindness are truly contagious. You have one of the sweetest souls, and your positivity always lifts our spirits. Thank you for understanding our vision and goals and for always standing by our side!

To the rest of the Clarkson Potter team, we are forever grateful for your support! A heartfelt thank-you to our publicist, Natalie Yera-Campbell, and our marketing expert, Stephanie Davis. To our new editor, Susan Roxborough: Thank you for graciously stepping in with kindness and support. To Elaine Hennig, our invaluable editorial assistant; Patricia Shaw, our diligent production editor; and Kim Tyner, our exceptional production manager, thank you for being part of what we consider to be our dream team!

Eva Kolenko: From the moment we saw the images you captured, we knew you were the one to bring our vision to life. Your talent behind the camera is truly remarkable, and the stories you weave with your pictures are nothing short of incredible. Working with you has been an absolute privilege; we are so thankful for the opportunity.

Natalie Drobny and Genesis Vallejo: Thank you for the energy you brought on set every single day!

Paige Arnett and Allison Fellion: Thank you for your tireless hours in the kitchen. We all know the easy part is the end result, but you helped make the process effortless from the start.

Mike Zielonka: Thank you for pushing boundaries, supporting us throughout this process, and always ensuring that Food Dolls was taken care of, especially during the busiest times of the cookbook. We are deeply grateful!

To our amazing Food Dolls team: You guys kept our blog thriving while we poured our hearts into this book. A huge thank-you to Lindsay Hardin, Jennifer Waldera, Shyanne Gregg, and Cory Aldinger. We truly couldn't have done it without you!

Mom: To say that we wouldn't be the women we are today if it weren't for you would be an understatement. You taught us to work hard and put our passion into everything that we do. Thank you for always being our biggest cheerleader, encouraging us at every turn. From teaching us the importance of family gathered around the dinner table to creating countless memories filled with laughter, tears, and love, you've shaped us in more ways than we can express. This book is a tribute to you, Mom, with heartfelt gratitude for all you've done. We love you.

Dad: Words can never describe how incredibly grateful we are for you. You dedicated your whole life to making sure that we were always taken care of. You've been our constant support through every triumph and trial. We've seen the courage and resilience you and Mom displayed as immigrants in a new land, forging a path for our better future. Your love and support mean everything to us. We love you! Thank you, Dad.

To the rest of our family and friends: We want to extend our heartfelt thanks to each and every one of you—for always listening, for trying out our recipes, and for sharing your wonderful feedback. Your unwavering support and encouragement mean everything to us. We have been so grateful to have you by our side. From the bottom of our hearts, thank you.

Our community: We will forever be grateful for your love and support. You have welcomed us into your homes and allowed us to be a small part of your lives. Our goal has always been to take the guesswork out of mealtimes, and we hope you enjoyed eating the meals as much as we enjoyed creating them. Your support is the spice that keeps us going!

From Alia

Radwa: If you had asked me ten years ago where we'd be today, I never would have imagined us creating a cookbook together. It seemed like something beyond our reach, but we didn't let that stop us! I'm so grateful we've shared this experience; we've laughed, cried, and stressed together, and I wouldn't want it any other way. Thank you for always encouraging us to try new things, even if they sound crazy! We've tested the most outrageous recipes together, and yet we created some of the best recipes! I love you and can't wait to see what we do next!

Riz: Thank you for always being there to help, whether it's taste-testing a pot de crème fifty times until we can't tell the difference, giving honest feedback, or simply lending a hand whenever I need it. You've been my rock and confidant throughout this entire process, and I can't thank you enough. I love you more than words can express.

Zain, Omar, and Adam: You've been with us since the beginning of this journey, witnessing all the hard work and dedication that went into creating this cookbook. I know tasting chocolate chip cookies was probably your favorite part, but I hope having witnessed all the mistakes and recipe fails only inspires you to keep trying even when things feel impossible. Here's to many more delicious meals and happy memories. I hope you share this book with your families and cook, create, love, and laugh with them, just like we do. Love you always!

From Radwa

Alia: This journey has taught us the true meaning of "never say never." I can't believe we created a cookbook together. Through all the laughter, excitement, hardships, and tears, I can't imagine having embarked on this adventure with anyone else. Thank you for always listening, even when my ideas were far-fetched. We've grown and evolved together in so many ways. You are not just my sister, but you are my built-in bestie. I love you and I'm incredibly proud of what we've accomplished together.

Rafiq: I couldn't have gotten here without your support and encouragement. Thank you for always being there when I need you, ready to help with anything. Even on those days when I'm completely wiped out, you're there, taking on the dishes (admit it, you love it!). Thank you for your willingness to taste-test anything, even right after breakfast. I'm so grateful for you and feel incredibly lucky to have you as my partner. I love you forever.

Maya and Lily: Thank you for the incredible gift of being your mom! You girls have brought indescribable joy into our lives. I love the memories we've spent making crazy messes in the kitchen and having fun baking together. I love your curiosity about the recipes in this book, even when you aren't sure about them! I hope this cookbook becomes a treasure that you both share with your families, continuing to create beautiful memories just as we have. From the bottom of my heart, I love you forever.

Index

Note: Page references in *italics* indicate photographs.

Published in the United States by Clarkson Potter/Publishers, an
imprint of the Crown Publishing Group, a division of Penguin
Random House LLC, New York.
ClarksonPotter.com

CLARKSON POTTER is a trademark and POTTER with colophon
is a registered trademark of Penguin Random House LLC.

Library of Congress Cataloging-in-Publication Data is available
upon request.

ISBN 978-0-593-79697-9
Ebook ISBN 978-0-593-79698-6

Printed in China

Editor: Raquel Pelzel
Editorial assistant: Elaine Hennig
Art director/designer: Marysarah Quinn
Production editor: Patricia Shaw
Production manager: Kim Tyner
Compositor: Merri Ann Morrell
Food stylist: Natalie Drobny
Food stylist assistants: Paige Arnett, Allison Fellion
Prop stylist: Genesis Vallejo
Prop stylist assistant: Catherine McGinty
Copy editor: Kate Slate
Proofreaders: Mark McCauslin, Kim Lewis,
   Sigi Nacson
Indexer: Elizabeth T. Parson
Publicist: Natalie Yera-Campbell
Marketer: Stephanie Davis

10 9 8 7 6 5 4 3 2 1

First Edition